Trauma and Grace

Trauma and Grace

Theology in a Ruptured World

SERENE JONES

WJK WESTMINSTER
JOHN KNOX PRESS
LOUISVILLE · KENTUCKY

© 2009 Serene Jones

First edition
Published by Westminster John Knox Press
Louisville, Kentucky

09 10 11 12 13 14 15 16 17 18—10 9 8 7 6 5 4 3 2 1

Except as otherwise noted, Scripture quotations are from the New Revised Standard Version of the Bible, copyright © 1989 by the Division of Christian Education of the National Council of the Churches of Christ in the U.S.A., and used by permission.

Chapter 1, "Trauma and Grace—Beginnings," was originally published in Yale Divinity School's *Spectrum* magazine (vol. 91, no. 1) and is used herein with the permission of Yale Divinity School Publications.

Chapter 2, "9/11's Emmaus: Gracing the Disordered Theological Imagination," was originally published in the *Union Quarterly Review* in 2002 and is used herein with the permission of Serene Jones.

Chapter 7, "Sin, Creativity, and the Christian Life: Rachel and Mary in Traumatic Embrace," was delivered as a shared lecture with Cindy Rigby at Princeton Theological Seminary in 2003 and then jointly authored and published in *The Princeton Seminary Bulletin* (25, no. 3 [2004]) and is used herein with the permission of *The Princeton Seminary Bulletin*.

Book design by Drew Stevens
Cover design by Night & Day Design
Cover art © Dinodia Photo Library/Brand X/Corbis

Library of Congress Cataloging-in-Publication Data

Jones, Serene, 1959–
   Trauma and grace : theology in a ruptured world / Serene Jones.
     p. cm.
   ISBN 978-0-664-23410-2 (alk. paper)
   1. Post-traumatic stress disorder—Patients—Religious life. 2. Post-traumatic stress disorder—Religious aspects—Christianity. 3. Psychic trauma—Religious aspects—Christianity. 4. Spiritual healing. 5. Psychology, Religious. 6. Suffering—Biblical teaching. I. Title.
   BV4910.45.J66 2009
   234—dc22

2009014231

PRINTED IN THE UNITED STATES OF AMERICA

♾ The paper used in this publication meets the minimum requirements of the American National Standard for Information Sciences—Permanence of Paper for Printed Library Materials, ANSI Z39.48-1992.

Westminster John Knox Press advocates the responsible use of our natural resources. The text paper of this book is made from 30% postconsumer waste.

Contents

Introduction

This book is a series of both published and new essays that explore recent works in the field of trauma studies and its critical and constructive relation to religious understandings of the nature of the self and salvation. Central to the overall theme is an investigation of the myriad ways both individual and collective violence affect a person's capacity to know, to remember, to act, and to love, and how those various circumstances potentially challenge theological understandings of how grace is experienced, how Jesus' death is remembered, and how the ethical character of Christian practice is assessed. Attention is given specifically to the long-term effects of collective violence on abuse survivors, war veterans, and marginalized populations and to the discrete ways in which grace and redemption might be articulated in each context. Materials are drawn from the social sciences, postmodern philosophy, and contemporary literature as well as from traditional theological sources and my own everyday pastoral experiences.

The essays do not offer answers—at least not in any straightforward way—to hard questions about the relationship between violence and redemption. Instead, they are a collection of epiphanic stories in which narratives of trauma, tales of grace, and the wisdom of doctrine are evocatively juxtaposed to provoke insight and stir imagination. As such, they are best viewed as a series of theological poems, albeit of a rather scholarly variety. Woven together, they exemplify the scattered, rich ways people grapple with the profound existential and moral questions raised by experiences of overwhelming violence and their long-term effects on communal and personal formation— and the reality of the grace that exists in the midst of it all. On the more academic side, they also attend to the methodological challenges of using social, scientific, and literary material as sources for systematic theological reflection and constructive doctrine, and to the knotty doctrinal challenges they substantively raise.

I began working in the field of trauma more by accident than by careful intention. Like so many pastors and professors I know, I have spent years worrying about students, family, friends, neighbors near and far, and community members whose lives had been so dramatically undone by violence that, try as they may, they could not seem to get the existential foothold on life that they needed to become active church participants and productive theology students, to say nothing of becoming generally happy people. It is an age-old worry, to be sure, but one that grew in intensity for me as my work took me to places as diverse as a village in India, a strategic hamlet in the Philippines, a sweatshop in Seoul, a domestic violence center in New Haven, and perhaps most challenging of all, the strange world of my students' own interior lives, a place where again and again I found tales of the past experience of violence that simply would not go away. In the midst of this, a decidedly nontheological friend of mine quite nonchalantly placed a book on trauma theory in my hands, and as I moved into its pages, the world around me began to look different. It was through this friend's offering in 1992 that I found the lens I needed to think about these experiences in a more informed and intellectually productive manner.

The question that drives these essays was formulated in those early days of reading trauma theory, and it has remained with me throughout the ten years it took to finish this book. It is simple in form but complex in content: *How do people, whose hearts and minds have been wounded by violence, come to feel and know the redeeming power of God's grace?* At the heart of this question sits a vexing problem: When people are traumatized, a kind of cognitive/psychic overwhelming breakdown can occur. When this happens, it becomes difficult for victims to experience the healing power of God's grace because their internal capacities (where one knows and feels) have been broken. It is hard to know God when your knowing faculties have been disabled. It is hard to feel divine love when your capacity to feel anything at all has been shut down. Addressing this vexing challenge is the core aim of the book.

Over the decade that I worked on this material, I amassed many narratives related to trauma and grace and how they relate to one another—tales taken from Scripture, from the weekly headlines, from the lives of students and friends. When strung together, these narratives also tell the story of my own circuitous journey through this complicated, vexing terrain. As much as possible, I have tried to retain the original voice of each essay because it carries something of my own unfolding bewilderment and confusion about trauma and my own dependence upon the wisdom of the communities in which these thoughts were formulated. The stories I tell are of the very real violence experienced by people I have come into contact with, though in many cases I have rewritten details of these narratives to protect the privacy of those involved. Just as trauma/violence is always excruciatingly particular in its form, and just as grace is always vibrantly particular in its shape, so too these essays try to maintain the integrity of the moments that provoked them. And as you will see, by entering the trenches of traumatic stories and theory, my own mind was forever changed and continues even now to change.

Yet there are some things that I have not changed my mind about: at the heart of each essay stand two deeply interrelated faith claims that are central to my understanding of Christian theology. First, we live in a world profoundly broken by violence and marred by harms we inflict upon each other. Second, God loves this world and desires that suffering be met by hope, love, and grace. Across the centuries, an ongoing challenge for the church has been to discern how this divine desire to love and heal can be spoken and lived out, concretely, in the life of faith at work in the world; this is the question of how God's love might best be embodied in tangible forms that can be felt, known, and enjoyed. In these essays, I suggest that understanding these harms as traumatic helps in this process, not only by expanding our appreciation for the complexities of human suffering, but also by deepening and enlivening our grasp of the amazing fullness and power of grace.

Helping pastors, parishioners, and students of theology understand the complexities of the human soul by helping them to think in fresh ways, not just about trauma but also about grace, is one of the larger purposes of collecting these essays and lectures in one place. By understanding in quite specific ways what trauma can do to the human person, we can better know what kind of thought patterns and bodily habits might help us to reimagine a better future. With this kind of knowledge, we might be better able to touch traumatized imaginations so that someone can rediscover old habits of imagination or reinvent new ones. It is hard to think of a task more central to Christian theology as a whole than this one: finding the language to speak grace in a form that allows it to come toward humanity in ways as gentle as they are profound and powerful.

I hope that by the end of this book, readers will have been provoked to find traces of this language in their own experiences—and in doing so, to think far beyond the borders of this book, thus to develop better ways of understanding the reality of "trauma" and "grace" in their own lives and the lives of friends and neighbors on a local and global scale. In addition to sharpened sight, I also hope that they might be inspired to think in practical ways about how grace might be concretely enacted or performed in people's lives. Like a furnace, there is no end to the flames that violence throws out, and the stories of harm that mark our individual and collective lives are as endless in variety as they are in scope. However, I ardently believe that the reality of grace is vastly richer and far more powerful than the force of those flames. It is so strong that even when our capacity to narrate the good-news story of grace is destroyed (as it often is in situations of violence), the reality to which it witnesses, the unending love of God, remains constant and steady and ever true.

A BRIEF SYNOPSIS OF THE CHAPTERS

The essays that follow are organized into three sections. Part 1 includes three early essays that introduce the concept of "trauma" and illustrate why it is useful to pastors and theologians who are interested in addressing the needs and concerns of people whose lives have been undone by violence. Chapter 1, "Trauma and Grace—Beginnings," was first published in Yale Divinity School's *Spectrum* magazine. It tells of my encounter with a young woman I call Leah; my church had appointed me to mentor her toward baptism. I discover that Leah suffers from post-traumatic stress disorder (PTSD) as the result of an early childhood trauma, and I wrestle with what it would take for the church to engage this kind of trauma as its social problem. I suggest that such an engagement requires not just a policy response but also a dramatic rethinking of our most basic categories and rituals—a reconstruction of imagination. I also argue that nestled in the practices and passions of historic Christianity are positive resources for addressing these harms and that by actively reclaiming them, we might be better able to help Christians to speak a word of hope to the traumatic realities that haunt our congregations—and the world—still today.

Chapter 2, "9/11's Emmaus: Gracing the Disordered Theological Imagination," continues this line of thought by moving from the tale of an individual trauma to a large-scale, collective one: the events of 9/11. The essay was first published in the *Union Quarterly Review* after being delivered as a lecture at Saint Paul's School of Theology the week after the devastating bombings occurred. It reflects my own disorientation amid the national disaster from which I—and the audience of my lecture—were still reeling. I show how the event disordered our collective psychic imagination by profoundly challenging our sense of safety and of orderly life. Against this backdrop, I use the story of the road to Emmaus as a tale that might usefully guide us forward. I suggest that the disciples on the road could not see Jesus walking with them because they were psychically caught in the feedback loop of the violence they had just experienced. Because the trauma of Jesus' execution had so truncated their vision, they were unable to see the gift of grace even when it walked right beside them. In conclusion, I suggest that now, eight years after the event, we as a nation continue to hold on to the truncated vision and hence remain caught in its traumatic repetition through our military presence in Iraq and Afghanistan. Thus I ask what it might take for us to see the grace that walks right next to us—and to manifest its strength in our international policies as well as our sermons.

Chapter 3, "Soul Anatomy: The Healing Acts of Calvin's Psalms," brings together the individual trauma of chapter 1 and collective trauma of chapter 2 and pulls both of them into conversation with a classical text in Christian theology, John Calvin's *Commentary on the Psalms*. It begins with the story of my downtown New Haven church struggling with the trauma induced by a drive-by shooting and the suffering of the child who witnessed it. I reflect on the fact that wrestling with violence like this has long been a challenge for the church, and that theologians like John Calvin have resources, well honed over time, for helping us cope. I describe the traumatic character of Calvin's sixteenth-century Geneva, focusing particularly on his small church, a community where the pastors and parishioners were being burned at the stake and hanged. Against this backdrop, I introduce his *Commentary on the Psalms* as a pastorally astute meditation on God's presence amid such violence. Using Judith Herman's account of the three stages of traumatic healing—establishing safety, hearing the story, integration into everyday life—I show that Calvin follows three similar steps in working with psalms of deliverance, psalms of lament, and psalms of thanksgiving. The essay concludes with reflections on how performing the Psalms in weekly church services might be a continued source of grace bestowed in the community today.

In part 2, I turn from the general topic of trauma to more focused theological reflections on the cross, one of the toughest themes I have wrestled with in my work on trauma. In chapter 4, I begin with a brief meditation on "The Alluring Cross," a Lenten theme that highlights the multiple ways the cross garners meaning in the imagination of those who behold it. In chapter 5, "The Mirrored Cross," I put flesh on these insights by turning to a group of women from the battered women's shelter who sat with me through the passion play in my church's Maundy Thursday service. Asking the questions: Why did they like the crucifixion so much? How did it work in their imaginations? I sketch out two trauma-informed images of the cross: the mirrored cross and the holographic cross. Then I add one more image to my gallery of trauma crosses: in chapter 6, "The Unending Cross," I explore the original ending of the Gospel of Mark, in which the women flee the empty tomb and tell no one. Using trauma theory, I suggest that their silence is the fractured speech of violence as it lives in their bodies and psyches, and I argue that their inability to speak parallels the experience of trauma survivors for whom speech, memory, and agency have been undone by violence. I further suggest that we resist giving Mark a cohesive ending but instead use his non-ending to remind us that, in a world filled with vast and unresolved traumas, Jesus comes to us anyway, in the midst of our faltering speech, our shattered memories, and our frayed sense of agency. This is truly what grace is, in its most radical form: not the reassuring ending of an orderly story, but the incredible insistence on love amid fragmented, unraveled human lives.

In part 3, I turn from the cross and begin to discuss more specifically the theme of grace. Chapter 7, titled "Sin, Creativity, and the Christian Life: Rachel and Mary in Traumatic Embrace," was delivered as a shared lecture with Cindy Rigby at Princeton Theological Seminary in 2003 and then jointly authored and published in *The Princeton Seminary Bulletin* (25, no. 3 [2004]). It is an imagined conversation between two women who encounter each other on the road leading away from the scene of Christ's crucifixion: Mary the mother of Jesus and Rachel, a woman I imagine into being whose son was executed by Roman soldiers in the slaughter of the innocents thirty years earlier. The essay explores how the tremendous loss suffered by both women not only causes them to grieve deeply, but also undoes their capacity to imagine a future and to see themselves as effective agents in the world. In other words, it undoes their sense of self. To move forward, their realities require redress in the form of a new story of self, a story that is, at its core, an embodied tale of grace. To tell this story, we offer a systematic theological account of what grace is and how it provides for each woman, differently, a sheath that enables her traumatic experience to be embraced and perhaps even healed.

Chapter 8, "Hope Deferred: Theological Reflections on Reproductive Loss," grew out of my participation in a group of women theologians gathered to reflect on the failure of the church to speak in theologically pertinent ways to people who have suffered the traumatic loss of a hoped-for child. The chapter centers on a painful evening I spent with a friend who asked me to help her deal with a recent miscarriage, not too long after I had suffered one. I muse on the inability of feminists to think about this loss as real because of the constraints placed on our discourse by the abortion debate and by the failure of Christian communities to face what happens to a woman's sense of identity when her body—her womb—becomes a living grave. In the conclusion I explore how this experience gives us new eyes to understand the cross and the Trinitarian life of God as one in which death happens within God and yet does not completely kill God—when God's body becomes a grave. Drawing on the images of the previous chapter, grace is again imagined in images of holding and beholding.

In chapter 9 I conclude with an exploration of the sin-grace theme running through this book, what it helps and how it harms; I suggest that perhaps habits of heart and imagination, rather than grand doctrinal stories, must carry the weight of our hopes for healing. I return as well to the theme of poetry, suggesting that instead of a grand narrative of redemption crafted to follow the driving-forward movement of the gospel story, we might be better served, when looking for the grace that heals, by poetry, a gappy, airy, disjunctive, associative genre well suited to the mirroring, holding, mourning, opening gestures described in earlier chapters. I also speak again of Leah, chapter 1's central figure, and I use her speech to provoke an exploration of the work of the French feminist Luce Irigaray, who describes the subject position of the "feminine" in Western culture as a site of violence, a traumatic self. I suggest that the story of the self undone by violence is described by her most powerfully in her reading of Teresa of Avila's essay "La mystérique," about the woman who crawls into the wound of Christ. I expand upon this image to suggest an alternate story of the self surprised by wonder, drawing on her reading of Descartes, and ending with a biblical reflection on the angel who asks the shepherds to "behold" the splendor of God.

ACKNOWLEDGMENTS

The thanks due to those who have helped with this book are far, far too numerous to name or, for that matter, even remember. Each essay had hosts of provoking angels calling it forth and tugging it toward completion. Classes filled with students, conferences filled with critically supportive colleagues, church committees populated with patient parishioner-friends, family members who couldn't wait for me to stop talking about a topic as cheery as trauma, and numerous readers/editors/staff who gave artful form to my often traumatically ill-formed thoughts—thank you for all the good stuff you so generously offered in the form of your own life stories and your ever more rich theological insights. You may find your stories unrecognizable in my fictionalized retelling of them, but I hope that at least the spirit of the original events rings true. I take full responsibility for the not-so-good parts of what came of it all. And particularly to those of you who told me to stop trying to find an answer and instead write essays/poems about the wrestling: you were right. The lilt of grace is far more interesting in its varied turns and slants of light than any answer we imagine.

PART 1

Traumatic Faith

Understanding the effects of violence upon the workings of our imagination—and upon the bodies and souls of persons who have been traumatized—is the central task of this opening section. Too often we believe that when physical healing occurs, mental healing naturally follows, and that with time, all wounds heal. Such is not always the case, however. Violence often cuts so deeply into our minds that surface healings cover it over and, hidden away, allow it to expand. The balmlike work of theology and of religion is to uncover and mend such wounds. And what medicine does this? Healing lies as much, if not more, in the stories we tell and the gestures we offer as in the doctrines we preach.

1
Trauma and Grace—Beginnings

BROKEN COMMUNION: LEAH'S STORY

Late to church as usual, I took a seat in the back pew. Leah, who had started attending services only six months ago, soon joined me. Quiet and intense, she had recently asked if I would be her official church-appointed sponsor because in several weeks she planned to join the congregation. As we discussed her life, her faith, and her decision to become a church member, a friendship had taken root.

When she sat down in the pew next to me, I smiled at her and we let ourselves be drawn into the familiar rhythms of worship. We stood and sang of God's glory; we sat and prayed for the world and ourselves; we listened to Scripture and then the sermon; we gave up our offerings and then rose to sing again. It was an ordinary Sunday morning: two friends, a familiar liturgy, and the calming power of prayer, silence, and song illuminated by the slant of midwinter light filtering through the sanctuary windows high above us.

After the offering, our pastor moved to the communion table. Since childhood, this part of the service has been my favorite; I like the image of Jesus gathering folks for supper and offering the mystery of God's grace to us in bread and wine. But as the pastor began talking about the night "before Jesus' death," Leah's body grew rigid. Her nail-bitten fingers began to twist the folded order of worship paper in her lap, her face assumed a frighteningly blank look, her fear was cold and palpable. When the pastor then invoked the words of Jesus, "This is my blood, poured out for you," she slid out of the pew and left the sanctuary. As I turned to see the back doors close softly behind her, I heard the pastor intone, "And this is my body, broken for you."

I followed her into the back hall and found her just inside the open door of the bathroom, where she stood shivering and staring at the sink. I stepped inside and asked her if she was all right. She looked over at me and haltingly said that she needed to put a little water on her face, . . . but she couldn't remember which faucet was hot and which was cold. It was such a simple thing—how could she not know? Before I answered, I tried to imagine what she might be thinking and why she was so afraid. For a moment, I felt the tightening grip of the terror that held her, and I seemed to be standing beside her—not in church, but in a chilling, static, confused world. We seemed far removed from the grace spoken about at the communion table and far from the warmth of the church that, literally, still held us deep inside itself.

After a few seconds, I turned on the hot water faucet for her. When the warm water finally came through the pipes, Leah put her wrists under it and slowly relaxed. We stepped back into the hall as the service ended. Leah found her coat, said good-bye, and moved outside into the late Sunday morning light as I stood there, now speechless myself, unnerved and guiltily uncertain about what had just happened or what I should have done.

❧❧❧❧❧

My anxious uncertainty was not just personal; it was also theological. I was her mentor, and the fact that the communion service had sent her running from worship troubled me to no end. How was it that the very thing she was reaching for was the thing that so terrified her? I knew from her talks with me about her faith that coming to know grace—God's unmerited love for her—was central to Leah's growing sense of spiritual connection with the church. Just the week before, we had talked long into the evening about grace and God's desire that she flourish and know the fruits of life abundant, a concept that was new to her but one to which she was rapidly warming. This week, however, a story-ritual about Jesus' love for her, grace incarnate, had thrown her into a cold, frightening place where violence seemed to stalk her. How could this be? How might the church not harm her in the very same moment it is trying to convey to her the treasure of a love unending?

The next time Leah and I met for afternoon tea, as was our custom, she shared with me the story of her childhood, a tale that threw light on why she had fled but not necessarily on the theological challenge of supporting her spiritual formation. As she told it, her parents had been hippie types in the early 1970s; until she was five, they had lived in a tent and traveled around the country with a caravan of folks, doing drugs and picking up short-term work here and there. During that period she remembered "lots of weird sex stuff and lots of stoned people frightening me as they stumbled around at night." When her family finally settled down, her father began sexually abusing her on a regular basis. "We were a liberated family," she sarcastically informed me. Her parents split up when she was in junior high; by the time she reached high school, she was doing drugs herself, trying to be cool. She was raped during her senior year, by a supposed friend; they had been drunk, and she never told anyone. By the time she started junior college, she was "too depressed to do much." With the help of a teacher, she had ended up at a community center, joining a group for young women. It was here, she explained, that she first heard a social worker use the word "trauma." She had gradually come to see that "trauma" fit the way she felt most of the time, that her whole self—her body and her soul—still held within it the shock waves of the violence she had known for so many years.

Since that time, she had been in and out of various treatment programs for people who suffer from what is called post-traumatic stress disorder (PTSD), in which they remain haunted by the ongoing effects of violence in their lives long after the events themselves have passed. Sometimes she felt she was getting better; at other times, she despaired about the future, including times like that Sunday when, out of the blue, she was suddenly thrown back into an old state of terror and confusion, which she could not stop or control. Afterward she had gone home and made razor-blade scratches on her arm, a ritual action that, she admitted with embarrassment, restored order to her world.

She took a sip of tea and said softly, "I'm sorry about church. I didn't mean to act so weird. I hate feeling so out of control." I assured her that there was no need to apologize and that I was sorry about the violence she had experienced: "It must have been horrible." My words sounded insignificant in the face of what she had revealed, but I didn't know what else to say. Once again, I was the one who felt frozen. She, however, looked relieved and rested her arms on the table as she continued her tale.

"I started coming to church when I moved into the city last year because I was lonely and—this may sound strange—but I really wanted to be in a place where I could do things like sing and pray with other people. And be with God." Growing up, her family had not been particularly religious, except for the few times when her mother, in brief fits of spiritual fervor, had taken her to a nearby church. She remembered how much she liked the hymns and hearing people lift up prayers to God. She told me that now she sometimes awakened in the morning with one of those songs rolling gently through her mind, its rhythm comforting her. Sometimes, too, out of nowhere, she found herself intoning small prayers that came from a deep place within her.

She then looked back into her teacup on the table and tried to explain what had happened the previous week:

It happens to me, sometimes. I'm listening to the pastor, thinking about God and love, when suddenly I hear or see something, and it's as if a button gets pushed inside of me. In an instant, I'm terrified; I feel like I'm going to die or get hurt very badly. My body tells me to run away, but instead, I just freeze. Last week it was the part about Jesus' blood and body. There was a flash in my head, and I couldn't tell the difference between Jesus and me, and then I saw blood everywhere, and broken body parts, and I got so afraid I just disappeared. I thought the bathroom might be safe, but even it scared and confused me. I forgot my name. I forgot the hot and cold.

She fell silent and started chewing on the side of her thumbnail. I tried to find words to reassure her, but she demurred: "I appreciate you listening, but . . . I know it's my problem, and I'm working on it."

"No," I responded quickly, words pouring out of my mouth before I even knew what I was saying. "It's not just your problem. It's our problem—my problem, the church's problem, God's problem. You don't need to be alone, and I hope we can work on it together. That's what faith communities do."

She eyed me with slight suspicion, for only a brief moment. The corner of her mouth tried a smile. Then she looked away and turned back to me with a new conversation topic.

❧❧❧❧❧

During the next few days, I found myself looking at people differently. As I gazed out into the classroom during my lecture, I wondered how many students had felt the traumatic reactions Leah described and how I might use the words of my teaching in a way that could better reach them. Over dinner with friends, I took a sip of wine and suddenly remembered Leah's story of rape. How many young women would be caught in a similar place tonight? I thought about Leah living in a tent: did she eat regular meals? These thoughts disturbed me and even reminded me of times in my own life. I was beginning to realize that Leah's terror had touched places in my own past that, while unlike hers in form, were hauntingly similar in feel. Trauma. In my mind, I began to see it everywhere.

I considered the promise I made to her about not going through it alone as she "worked on it." God, the church, and I could be with her. The more I thought about my urgently issued assurance, however, the less certain I was as to what I had meant by it. How could the church's profession of grace reach Leah in the cold space of her distress?

These questions came into particularly sharp focus for me at a meeting with a dozen church deacons convened to discuss fund-raising for the urgently needed renovation of a local soup kitchen. The conversation was lively, but instead of engaging in it, I listened and watched. Looking around the meeting room, I saw twelve familiar, concerned faces. Our church had a long history of engaging in social issues: homelessness, illiteracy, racism, hate crimes, hunger, AIDS, domestic violence. We were experts at setting up committees to investigate community problems and formulate effective plans of action. We didn't like walls that separated people from each other or walls that separated the church from the world around it. But what of the walls constructed inside the self and between Leah's terror and our songs of grace and mercy?

I was certain that if this group knew about Leah's experience, their faces would immediately be filled with earnest concern. But I feared that our response to it might be to form a social action committee. I was confident that such a committee could begin to address, as we already had, many of the social conditions that led to Leah's terror. But I wondered, Could a trauma committee do the work that would help Leah heal? I suspected not. Perhaps we needed to obtain therapy for her. But she clearly had had that and had chosen a church for other reasons. How could liturgy, community, and faith work together best to encourage healing in broken places?

The meeting came to a close; we decided to make renovating the kitchen a top priority. A good decision, I thought. But I walked away filled with worries about Leah and the church.

Worries about walls and about the absence of answers to my still unspoken questions about trauma and grace.

❖❖❖❖❖

The next week I arrived at church, late again, and was happy to see Leah already sitting in our usual pew. This morning, however, the routine felt different. Sitting next to Leah, I waited for even the smallest sign that something might be going wrong. I tried to imagine what the songs, prayers, silences, Scripture readings, and sermon might sound like to Leah. I tried to recall what I knew of traumas in my own life, what it felt like in my body to be terrified and confused. In a new way I was also aware of the people sitting in front of and behind me and what they might be thinking. Scattered around us were veterans, one from World War II, one from Vietnam, and another from Desert Storm. There was a mother whose son had died from driving drunk last spring, a fourteen-year-old girl who had witnessed a drive-by shooting and had testified about it in court, and a father who had emigrated recently from Rwanda, a place about which he seldom spoke. And there were others, I'm sure, who had suffered violent losses, some of whom had never spoken of them to anyone. "How did the Lord's Prayer sound to each of them?" I asked myself. "Did our collective words of thanksgiving to God make sense in the face of so much pain and loss?"

The whole world of worship as I had known it in the past began to shift and change before my eyes: there, in Center Church on the Green in New Haven, I came as close as a Congregationalist comes to having a mystical experience. The vision was powerful. A new world appeared before me. In it, we were still in the sanctuary, but Leah's cold, ice-white tiled bathroom had expanded to hold a whole congregation of shivering souls. It was a world in which I could not rely on normal assumptions about human perceptions and actions. Here memories were blurry. Commonly held notions of order, like the order of the hot and cold faucets, seemed unstable, elusive. Scenes of violence erupted without pattern, overwhelming both thought and sound. Bodies were frozen in fear, and a sense of utter helplessness filled the air. Mouths were gaping open in screams, but no sounds came out, no language worked. And cold blankness constantly threatened to descend.

What was most strange about this scene was that its chaos was unfolding not off in a corner bathroom but in the midst of worship itself. The belly-body of the sanctuary held all of it within its viscera; the liturgy moved in and through its midst, circulating through its aisles and around the many lives it held. At times, the words spoken, sung, or prayed struck violently against the fragile, traumatized people that gathered there, deepening the terror. I knew at once that such words and actions were not harbingers of grace but the spawn of the church's own brokenness and history of violence. I wanted to reach over and shield Leah from their assaultive force, to shelter her, others, myself.

At other times, however, our faith-born words and ritual motions seemed truly grace-filled as they circled around and through this frozen, terrified lot—powerful, merciful, and transforming. In an old hymn was a gentle plea for vision where only shadows haunted—a familiar song that sounded like the words of someone who had known a terror like Leah's. In the Gospel lesson, I heard anew the story of confused disciples who kept missing Jesus' message, disciples with whom he nonetheless kept traveling, warming them, feeding them, starting over again and again with his folksy version of the gospel tale. In all these ways, I heard and saw with increasing clarity that trauma was not something outside of faith, something foreign and distant that the Christian message of grace had to struggle to address. I saw instead that parts of our rich faith traditions were born in the midst of unspeakable terrors and that grace had long been unfurling its warmth and succor therein.

The Gospel of Mark calls it "repentance"—that moment when one is turned around and sees differently. The apostle Paul speaks of it as conversion, transformation, and describes for us the new reality that opens up when one comes to know Christ and see him crucified. Augustine of Hippo speaks of the baptism of blood, that turbulent transformation in which one descends into death, perhaps into terror and cold blankness, and emerges in Christ. John Calvin calls it "mortification and vivification," a conversion in which one descends into hell to find life.

That morning, sitting next to Leah, I underwent such a baptism, a converted way of seeing. I had come to see that when one becomes aware of the extensive wounds that events of overwhelming violence can inflict on the souls, bodies, and psyches of people, one's understanding of what human beings are and what they can do changes. Dramatically. Such an experience shifts how one thinks about language and silence, how one understands the workings of memory, how one assesses the instability of reason and the fragility of our capacity to will and to act, how one grapples with the fragmentation of perception and the quick disintegration of order, and how one conceives of imagination, recognizing that at any moment haunting, shadowy scenes of violence can disrupt it, twist it, and shut it down.

The vision I had in church that morning is crucial to moving forward. If the church's message about God's love for the world is to be offered to those who suffer these wounds, then we must think anew about how we use language and how we put bodies in motion and employ imagery and sound. With fresh openness we must grapple with the meaning of beliefs not only about grace, but also about such matters as sin, redemption, hope, community, communion, violence, death, crucifixion, and resurrection.

The reality of violence haunts us all, daily, in varying ways and to varying degrees. When we turn on the evening news, we see buildings explode, nations dissolve, whole peoples disappear, millions die, and children lose their futures. The violence of our world is, in this regard, very visible and theologians often speak about it. What these news stories fail to show us in their pictures of devastated lives is the haunting reality that, for the living, violence often continues to exist and expand, in the recesses of their minds and in their patterns of action and of hoping. If faith tells us that God desires that we flourish, that we know the fruits of life abundant, then surely the church should be able to proclaim such grace in the midst of this often-hidden legacy of violence. But how? My guess is that there are many answers—and understanding what we can about trauma is an important early step in discovering what they might be.

DEFINING "TRAUMA"

Like many popular words used in our pastoral and theological texts, the term "trauma" has come to mean different things to different people. After Leah introduced me to the clinical concept of trauma, in such an up close and personal way, I began to read broadly in a field called trauma studies and have drawn from this literature a definition that is partly psychological and sociological, partly literary and poetic, and partly philosophical and theoretical. Given how vast these fields are, however, it is remarkable that there exists such consensus about the basic features of a traumatic event.

The ancient Greek word for trauma, τραῦμα, means a "wound" or "an injury inflicted upon the body by an act of violence." To be traumatized is to be slashed or struck down by a hostile external force that threatens to destroy you.[1] This visual image highlights the assaultlike character of a trauma; it involves an attack by an external agent upon a vulnerable human body in such a way that a wounding occurs.[2]

Although the Greek definition of "trauma" focuses primarily on physical wounds, contemporary trauma studies have extended its application to the mind and the emotions, focusing on the effects of violence on our vast interior worlds, or to use another ancient term, our psyches. The challenge of understanding this type of harm is that unlike external injuries, a wounded psyche doesn't always manifest the signs of harm or suffering we typically associate with violence. What the literature on trauma tells us, however, is that such harms are no less damaging than more visible ones. Like mortal wounds, they can destroy a human life, and precisely because they are invisible, they can do so in secret, hidden ways. In addition to a bleeding arm or a broken leg, violence can leave you with a wounded soul—a life marked by obsessive thoughts, acute anxiety, depression, dissociative states like Leah experienced, and low-grade forms of misery lingering so long that they become normalized and cease to appear woundlike at all.

That a violent event could do this to someone's internal spirit as well as their bodies, I believe, is hard to accept because it exposes how vulnerable we are, deep inside, to the many forms of violence that surround us and that we ourselves enact. The positive side of understanding these effects of traumas, however, is that by bringing them to light, we make them available for the balmlike work of human care and grace.

Central Features of Trauma

What are the primary characteristics of trauma? Before outlining its basic psychological features, it is helpful to look at the kind of event that can cause a traumatic reaction in someone. Two leading clinical psychologists who have studied trauma, Bessel van der Kolk and Judith Herman, tell us that understanding the anatomy of the original traumatic event helps throw light on the effects it generates. Doing so also helps us distinguish *trauma* from the more generally stressful or disturbing occurrences we all face in the course of daily life.

Here's how they characterize a traumatic event: "A traumatic event is one in which a person or persons perceives themselves or others as threatened by an external force that seeks to annihilate them and against which they are unable to resist and which overwhelms their capacity to cope." Several features stand out in this characterization.

First, traumatic events are distinguishable in their order of magnitude. They are not events that simply make one feel unhappy or uncomfortable or even profoundly sad or griefstricken. They are, instead, events in which one experiences the threat of annihilation. One's continued existence is called into question by the specter of impending death or looming destruction. The scope of the threat is, in this sense, total. Life itself is at stake.

Second, such an event becomes traumatic for a person only when it is internally, subjectively experienced as such. In other words, it has to mentally register or to be "perceived" or "imagined" as life threatening in order for it to actually be experienced as traumatic. If one happens not to notice a near-miss car accident or is able to laugh after a seven-year-old's foot knocks out a tooth, then chances are that the event will not wound the psyche in a traumatic way.

Third, this subjective experience of potential annihilation is usually grounded in a real event of some sort, although one's memory of it can, at times, be unstable. In this regard, trauma is not simply a fictionally induced psychological state; it is embedded in lived relationships and provoked by concrete occurrences like those addressed in this book: sexual abuse, bombing, loss of a hoped-for child, a close friend's death by torture, genocidal rampage of sectarian nationalism, flood, car accident, fire.[3] These are not purely subjective events of spirit; they take place in the flesh and blood of everyday life as we know it.

Fourth, events can be traumatic for those who are not their immediate victims but nearby witnesses. Seeing a collapsing building kill hundreds or watching a beloved friend tortured to death (to use two examples from this book) are not necessarily life-threatening events for the people who witness them, but as these essays explore, the marks left upon the mind and heart of the witness can be as emotionally devastating as the physical wounds that were avoided. The sheer force of such violence, it seems, can collapse—at an experiential level—the distinctions we commonly make between "you and me." In so doing, the violence that undoes you becomes, quite literally, my own.

Fifth, violent events can befall both individuals and communities, both villages and nations, both single families and whole regions. This requires moving back and forth between single-person and collective events when thinking about the relation between trauma and grace, comparing the individual loss of a hoped-for child in suburban Connecticut, for example, to the state-sanctioned murder of hundreds in an ancient Palestinian township. Though it is useful to keep these distinctions in mind—the individual and the collective are not the same—it is remarkable how many traumatic features they share. For instance, just like a person, a country can lose its memory. Or just like a city, a person can try to set up impenetrable borders in response to fear of assaulting invasion.

Sixth, traumatic events are not necessarily limited to one-time occurrences of cataclysmic proportions; they can also be repeated events of the low-intensity variety, like the constant threat of violence in some forms of domestic abuse or hostile workplace environments. In such instances, the assault on the psyche is no less disabling than a frontal attack; but because it never reaches the explosive level of violence we associate with traumatic harm, its corrosive effects are more likely to go unnoticed—and uninterrupted—for years.

Seventh, traumatic events are "overwhelming" insofar as they are experienced as inescapable and unmanageable. They outstrip our capacity to respond to and cope with them. Like the wave of a tsunami, they drown you and disable your normal strategies for dealing with difficulties. You lose a sense of yourself as someone who can take effective action against an attacking agent, because at a literal level, either you cannot fight back, or if you do, you fail. These events also overwhelm your capacity to make intelligible sense of them because they are stronger and more intense than the best meaning-making strategy you have. In this regard, they override your powers of both action and imagination.

By understanding the scope and magnitude of a traumatic event, we can already see many of the effects it causes: a loss of a sense of self, a breakdown in normal knowing and feeling, and a paralyzing lack of agency in the threat of the harm suffered. The magnitude of these events is such that the effects they produce, like a grievous physical wound, can remain and fester long after the initial harm.

PTSD: Defining Post-Traumatic Stress Disorder

Not everyone who undergoes a violent event necessarily suffers long-term psychological damage from it; yet too often the pain and shock it provokes lingers long after the event has passed. In clinical literature, this lingering condition is referred to as post-traumatic stress disorder (PTSD); according to the National Institute of Mental Health, it currently affects about 7.7 million American adults. Several symptoms are associated with the disorder, some of which inform the essays in this book, albeit translated into my own rather loose, nonclinical descriptions.

First, people with PTSD are excessively vigilant when it comes to monitoring their external environment and are easily startled by loud noises and sudden movements. They are always preparing for the next attack, as it were, by keeping their sensory and cognitive functions in a state of *hyperarousal*. Such vigilant attention can make them jumpy, edgy, and nervous, as with Leah that morning in worship. She was startled and terrified when an organ blast announced the hymn.

Second, this state can be intermingled with feelings of *numbness* and emotional or cognitive deadness. Physiologically, this can include feeling disconnected from the body, feeling psychologically as though you have detached from yourself, or viewing your experiences as if they were happening at a distance or you were floating somewhere above them. In Leah's case, this state, clinically called *dissociation*, was manifest most vividly by the blank look on her face and her corresponding inability to feel hot and cold water.

Third, trauma survivors can suffer from acute anxiety and sleeplessness because of recurring, *intrusive memories* of the original traumatic event. These can take the form of nightmares but can also occur during waking hours when a violent scene suddenly flashes through the mind, throwing one momentarily back into a state of terror. A reaction like this was triggered, I am certain, in Leah when she heard the pastor speak of breaking the body of Christ. Suddenly she was caught up in a memory scene that took her far from the world of the pew we shared.

Fourth, survivors often suffer from unarticulated *compulsions to repeat* the event in different ways in the midst of their everyday life activities. This compulsion can lead survivors to put themselves in situations similar to the initiating event, as in the case of the sexual abuse survivor who repeatedly gets involved in abusive relationships, or the veteran who cannot help turning daily life activities into battlefield-intensity encounters. One can become something of a crisis junkie and find relief from inner turmoil by becoming involved in other people's chaos or continually creating one's own. Repetition can also occur in less obvious ways, as in the case of obsessive disorders where the original traumatic event serves as an unconscious template for anxiety-driven plays of mind and actions like cutting oneself, eating disorders, or substance abuse. Because such compulsions are not always conscious, victims describe themselves as "haunted" by feelings and associations that circulate through their interior worlds in a ghostlike manner, affecting everything but never appearing explicitly on the surface.

Fifth, trauma survivors suffer a *loss* or *diminishment* of both *memory* and routine *language use.* When I first came upon Leah in the bathroom, she could not recognize or speak coherently to me. Given the psychologically overwhelming nature of the violence, victims are often unable to fully register the event as it is happening to them and therefore may not fully remember it afterward, particularly if they were dissociated during its occurrence. Lost or fragmenting memory is also linked to an incapacity to express meaningful thoughts or speak comprehensively to others. Even simple words can fail trauma survivors, an experience that mirrors the fact that when they were violated, normal cognitive functions may have failed in a similar manner.

Sixth, alongside this breakdown of cognitive, linguistic function is an unraveling of agency; trauma survivors can lose confidence that they are effective actors in the world because, in the original event, they experienced just the opposite: a state of frozen *powerlessness*. They come to believe that their actions do not matter or cannot effect change. A state of deep passivity and depressive anxiety often follows. Along with this loss of will comes a *loss of hope*. Unable to act, one loses the desire to make future plans and execute them. In Leah's case, the simple act of turning on hot water became unimaginable not only because it required knowing which knob to turn but also because it assumed the ability to lift her hand and make it happen.

Seventh, these factors in combination create for trauma survivors what is perhaps the most insidious feature of PTSD: a sense of *isolation* from others and from their primary communities of affection and care. Because they have difficulty in speaking and remembering, trauma survivors find it hard to communicate with loved ones and friends. Because they lack energy or optimism, they find it tough to sustain relationships. And perhaps most poignantly, because a hostile external force has violated them, they find it hard to trust people; anyone who draws near to them could be a potential attacker. Further, others often find it uncomfortable to be around trauma survivors, and one thus finds a situation that is deeply conflicted: the very thing that one needs to heal, trusted and close relationships, requires engaging the reality that one fears most, other people.

In addition to these general features, trauma theorists remind us that the shape of traumatic violence is as intricately and inextricably individual as the complex lives it effects and the communities it undoes. For this reason, these outlined symptoms of PTSD rarely appear together, in pure form, in any one life or one place. In each case, its dimensions are unique and not easily transferable to other cases. When dealing with human suffering like this, the desire to dissect and measure its form and quantity is understandably strong—we want to avoid it as much as we want to cure it. Ultimately, however, our categorizations of it fall short because, finally, to be human is to live only a hairbreadth away from the unbearable.[4] This account of PTSD thus captures something of experiences that potentially plague us all.

TRAUMA AND GRACE:
A DISORDERED IMAGINATION

In the days and weeks that followed my initial encounter with Leah, she increasingly allowed me to see the inside of her interior life. For someone with no clinical training, learning the trials of PTSD from her was a gift beyond measure, a rare chance for me to be accompanied by a resident expert on my journey into the complex land of trauma, its lived form as well as the literature devoted to it. The images that she repeatedly offered in her accounts of a traumatic reaction were of *rupture* and *disorder*. She often depicted her internal world being suddenly "bombed" by an intrusive memory or "exploded and scattered" by a triggering moment (like communion); in an instant, she claimed, something could startle her, causing everything inside her mind to just fall apart—her memory, her language use, her capacity to keep track of time. All of these faculties would simply collapse. Similarly, she told me how painful it was for her to find violence stalking her not in real-life events, but in the constant "plays of mind" her brain would call up. Walking through the grocery store could easily become a scene as terrifying as being stalked in the park at midnight. Meeting a friend for lunch could quickly stir in her levels of anxiety reminiscent of a threatening rape scene. And so on. In her own language, she told me, "I can't control my own imagination—it does weird things to me. It freaks out. Gets all shattered and chaotic and plays out scenes I don't want."

She also added that part of the beauty and power of church for her was the comforting order that our stories and our order of worship provided for her. "The Bible stories, they are so alive and simple and good—it's like they override the bad stuff." It was not just the content of the stories, either. It was also their repetition and their constant reenactment, at an embodied level. "When I sing, I relax, especially if it's an old song I love. I don't even have to think about it. And praying, it's like a meditative exercise that slows down the chaos and stops the bad thoughts." In words that I found most telling of all, she described how the language of faith gave her a graced imagination: "It's like a poem that centers me and calms me down and gives me hope and makes everything feel so real." That was true except when the same words were causing her to emotionally shut down and run away, as she had that earlier Sunday during communion.

Building on these discussions with her, I began to think about theologically engaging the traumatized mind as a challenge of *healing imagination*. By "imagination" I do not mean to imply any complicated abstraction of experience; I use the word to refer to the fact that as human beings we constantly engage the world through organizing stories or habits of mind, which structure our thoughts. Our imagination simply refers to the thought stories that we live with and through which we interpret the world surrounding us. Imagination is an old category and raises interesting questions for us about the relationship between trauma and grace.

In his 1688 dissertation for the University of Basel, the physician Johannes Hofer wrote about trauma and imagination in helpful ways. He described what he found in patients mentally sickened by a violent event as a "disease of the visual mind":

> [It is a] disease that is due essentially to *a disordered imagination*, whereby the part of the brain chiefly affected is that part in which the images are located. This is the inner part of the brain where the vital spirits constantly surge back and forth through the nerve fiber in which the impressions are stored. Once the vital spirits have made a path for themselves and widened it, they find it easier, as in sleep, to take the same path, again and again.[5]

Although we have more sophisticated language to describe the workings of the brain today, Hofer's insight is still remarkably accurate with respect to what we know of trauma. A traumatic event reconfigures the imagination, affecting our ability to tell stories about ourselves and our world that are life giving and lead to our flourishing.

The following essays are my attempts to think through the implications of experiences like Leah's for the healing work of theology and faith communities today. The Christian faith provides a manner of imagining that inspires a way of life shaped deeply by biblical stories, rituals, and traditions, and it has its own ways of ordering the imagination. Though different strands of Christianity may form imaginations somewhat differently, there is a common imaginative landscape that most Christians inhabit. In that landscape agency, embodiment, diachronic time (the time of our real histories), coherence, and interrelation are central. A Christianly formed imagination thus tells stories about people who are agents in their own lives, with God-given grace to act, moving through concrete embodied history in time, coherently connected to their own pasts and the stories of others who came before them, related intimately to other people and to the good creation that sustains them, and looking forward in hope to a flourishing future. The challenge of these essays is to explore how an imagination shaped by grace might meet and heal an imaginative world disordered by violence.

This is a tall order, but we do not have to start from scratch. Christianity does not need to discern the relationship between trauma and grace from a blank slate; after all, it was founded on the story of the crucifixion and resurrection of Jesus. So in a very real way its central story is one of trauma and grace. In the same way, the church has struggled to speak to its believers for centuries—sometimes in successful ways, sometimes not so successfully. Maybe the fact that the liturgy affected Leah so strongly is the point. The language of faith can reach straight into the heart of the imagination. The fragmented anatomy of trauma can leave one without a world, without speech, stories, memory, community, future, or a sense of self; theology's task is to renarrate to us what we have yet to imagine. As Leah's story takes hold of our own psyches, we are reminded that these issues are particular not just to her, but also to everyone.

If grace has power to reshape the imagination, then theology is the language that both describes that power and evokes it in the lives of people by telling grace-filled stories of new imaginings. But just as the shattering effects of trauma are painfully particular to each person who suffers them, so the healing power of grace is specific to each imagination it soothes and heals. Recognizing this fact led me to abandon the project of writing a systematic theology of trauma and grace. Rather, what my own writings on trauma continue to seek is a glimpse of grace at work in the interstices of imagination. As for Leah, she and I continue to wrestle with many questions, both of us continually crafting and recrafting the language of love that works in the imaginative world of our particular lives. For me, that means crafting theological essays (like those collected in this volume), which I hope are, at best, simple and honest reflections on the reality of what it means to be human and hence, at core, creatures of imagination, both broken and graced. And perhaps, by grace, they are even honest reflections of the mysterious love of a God who desires to meet us in the concrete, historical, messy particularity of our lives

2

9/11's Emmaus

Gracing the Disordered Theological Imagination

On the morning of September 11, 2001, I was writing a lecture on the topic of trauma and violence for a presentation I was scheduled to make to pastors at St. Paul's School of Theology. I was pleased with the piece: it focused on some of the insights I had gleaned through my theological work with Leah. I was polishing it up when a colleague called and told me to turn on the television: I watched as a plane flew into the second World Trade Center tower.

In that moment, my nicely ordered talk, which had seemed so important just seconds earlier, felt inconsequential and crumbled in my hands. How could I speak about traumatic experiences and the Christian faith without speaking directly about these events? I knew immediately—or rather, as soon as my thoughts were able to return to this upcoming event—that I had to speak about what I saw before my eyes. But as every pastor who preached the week after the attacks knows, it is hard to write about traumatic events while still living in the rawness of their aftermath. Trauma never, at least not immediately, breeds a fine-tuned tongue or an exceptionally sharp eye.

In the days that followed, I rewrote the talk again and again, trying to keep pace with the changing international scene as well as the rapidly changing world of my own reactions and emotions. Every time I sat down to write, however, I was overwhelmed with feelings of confusion, a sense of uncertainty, blurriness; it was hard to breathe, and my stomach hurt. I knew it was crucial, in times like those, for powerful theological words to be spoken; but I, like so many others around the world, was scared and quite literally could not bring order to my thoughts. When I finally presented the lecture on September 18, it was still unfinished: the text was ragged, its words halting, its ideas scattered. I did not know then that the U.S. military would eventually go into not just Afghanistan but also Iraq and that the civilian toll of those events would reach beyond the bounds of any imagination. Nor did I know that the tales of trauma this event would continue to generate would be endless in both scope and detail. However, my reflections offered almost eight years ago in the immediate aftermath of trauma still seem to have something to say to the present, particularly concerning the question of collective trauma. In startling and painful ways, 9/11 is exemplary of the continued effects of trauma in communities around the world, and of our continued need to process it through acts of memory and imagination. The aim of this essay, as with the talk I delivered at St. Paul's at a moment that was much more immediate to the trauma of 9/11, is to prompt our imaginations to find new language for the long-term aftermath of a shared violence that has shaped our world.

I began the talk at St. Paul's with a story from Luke 24:13–43, the story of the <u>disciples on the road to Emmaus</u> and their encounter with Jesus. As I stepped into this story in the wake of 9/11, I could not help but see it as a tale of trauma and survival:

> Now on that same day two of them were going to a village called Emmaus, about seven miles from Jerusalem, and talking with each other about all these things that had happened.

While they were talking and discussing, Jesus himself came near and went with them, but their eyes were kept from recognizing him. And he said to them, "What are you discussing with each other while you walk along?" They stood still, looking sad. Then one of them, whose name was Cleopas, answered him, "Are you the only stranger in Jerusalem who does not know the things that have taken place there in these days?" He asked them, "What things?" They replied, "The things about Jesus of Nazareth, who was a prophet mighty in deed and word before God and all the people, and how our chief priests and leaders handed him over to be condemned to death and crucified him. But we had hoped that he was the one to redeem Israel. Yes, and besides all this, it is now the third day since these things took place. Moreover, some women of our group astounded us. They were at the tomb early this morning, and when they did not find his body there, they came back and told us that they had indeed seen a vision of angels who said that he was alive. Some of those who were with us went to the tomb and found it just as the women had said; but they did not see him." Then he said to them, "Oh, how foolish you are, and how slow of heart to believe all that the prophets have declared! Was it not necessary that the Messiah should suffer these things and then enter into his glory?" Then beginning with Moses and all the prophets, he interpreted to them the things about himself in all the scriptures.

As they came near the village to which they were going, he walked ahead as if he were going on. But they urged him strongly, saying, "Stay with us, because it is almost evening and the day is now nearly over." So he went in to stay with them. When he was at the table with them, he took bread, blessed and broke it, and gave it to them. Then their eyes were opened, and they recognized him; and he vanished from their sight. They said to each other, "Were not our hearts burning within us while he was talking to us on the road, while he was opening the scriptures to us?" That same hour they got up and returned to Jerusalem; and they found the eleven and their companions gathered together. They were saying, "The Lord has risen indeed, and he has appeared to Simon!" Then they told what had happened on the road, and how he had been made known to them in the breaking of the bread.

While they were talking about this, Jesus himself stood among them and said to them, "Peace be with you." They were startled and terrified, and thought that they were seeing a ghost. He said to them, "Why are you frightened, and why do doubts arise in your hearts? Look at my hands and my feet; see that it is I myself. Touch me and see; for a ghost does not have flesh and bones as you see that I have." And when he had said this, he showed them his hands and his feet. While in their joy they were disbelieving and still wondering, he said to them, "Have you anything here to eat?" They gave him a piece of broiled fish, and he took it and ate in their presence.

(Luke 24:13–43)

❧❧❧❧❧

The story of Cleopas on the road to Emmaus is amazing: it is the story of the agile, insistent presence of grace in our midst. In our contemporary world "our midst" includes, as it did for the disciples, the harsh reality of life in the aftermath of an event of overwhelming violence. What does this story tell us, then, about the relation between trauma and grace? How might this narrative give us the language to consider our collective, lived experience of violence in a post-9/11 United States? In the first section of the essay that follows, I consider the relation between individual and collective violence. In the second section, I ask: What does it mean to minister to people in the midst of such an immediately traumatized world? What is the church called to do and be in times of collective trauma? Finally, I conclude by examining some of the "solutions" we have been offered by popular culture to frame the violence of 9/11; I suggest alternative narratives available from the Christian tradition—from our repertoire of stories, images, and practices—that might help us imagine healing in the long aftermath of traumatic violence, without forgetting or ignoring that it has shaped who we are.

TRAUMA STUDIES

As we saw in the last chapter, scholars of trauma studies in a number of different fields have become interested in looking at how events of traumatic violence affect both individuals and communities and, in particular, how they influence the way people perceive and make meaning of their worlds after such events. Although the most well-known work in this field has been pursued by psychologists and psychotherapists, it extends more broadly as well. In literature departments, trauma theorists are looking at how violence affects the way we use words and images to represent such experiences. Sociologists and anthropologists are exploring not only how violence influences individual psyches, but also how whole communities, nations, and entire regions cope with the long-term effects of such violence, and specifically how it shapes their cultures and the images they use to make sense of and negotiate the world (one might think here of Iraq, Rwanda, Darfur, Ethiopia, Bosnia, South Africa, and Afghanistan). Building on this literature of collective trauma, historians are wrestling with legacies of violence and how such events continue to shape cultural imaginations and practices generations later, such as the legacy of chattel slavery in North America and its ongoing cultural realities. In law schools and political science departments, there is also new interest in grappling with the ways trauma challenges how we think about such things as the purpose of the law, the nature of "the citizen," the character of national identity, and the shape of political visions.

Running throughout these vast literatures are many important defining distinctions that are crucial to the field as a whole. As discussed in the previous chapter, theorists have identified a set of reactions that an individual often undergoes following trauma, now known as post-traumatic stress disorder (PTSD). Diagnostically, this disorder consists of symptoms such as memory loss, dissociative episodes, a profound sense of powerlessness, feelings of being haunted by intrusive memories and repetitive thought patterns, an ongoing state of hyperarousal, and perhaps most painfully, a loss of basic trust and the capacity to meaningfully relate to others. Because traumatic violence so decisively violates one's personal-physical-emotional borders, the desire to build emotional protective armor around oneself is all consuming and, sadly, results in a sense of dramatic isolation.

As the collective national experience of 9/11 so powerfully demonstrated, however, these symptoms do not just apply to individuals but apply to groups as well. On a grand scale, the way we experience ourselves as a community of thinkers, actors, and embodied agents could not help but be profoundly impacted by the events of 9/11. Without in any way minimizing the suffering of those whose bodies were literally torn apart by the event and those whose bodies and souls experienced direct violence in the immediate aftermath of 9/11, it is worth reflecting on how 9/11 as an event also drew the nation as a whole into the trauma drama of its violence. How do the symptoms of PTSD resonate with the experience of trauma we have undergone collectively since September 11?

A simple definition of a traumatic event is an experience in which a person perceives oneself or another to be threatened with annihilation. When I turned on the television on the morning of September 11, I and most of North America and indeed much of the world watched thousands of people die before our very eyes. We saw the real—not merely threatened or feared—annihilation of people who were or could have been our family, friends, neighbors, or parishioners. At first as I watched, I thought, "There are few people in the history of the world who have witnessed, in the moment of its occurrence, such massive death, a witnessing now made possible by our current telecommunications technology." As I continued to watch, the most powerful initial response these images triggered was incredulity, a sense of disbelief that anyone could actually be seeing this happen. The violence was stupefying. That is how trauma often feels in the space of its occurrence: It cannot be happening.

We can expand the definition of a traumatic event to say that
it provokes a feeling of utter helplessness on the part of the survivor: we can do nothing to stop the event. As I sat on my couch
that morning, the sense of powerlessness that overcame me was
palpable. I called my parents and sisters just to hear their voices
as I wandered around my house. It was the only act I could
perform. This feeling of powerlessness was directly related to
another part of the definition of trauma: traumatic events overwhelm a person's capacity to cope. What is coping if not the
ability to sift and sort through the information of daily experience in a way that allows it to make sense? As I watched the
images on my television, those structures of meaning collapsed.
It was as if the world as I had known it had come unhinged;
where there had been meaning, only a gaping hole remained.

As I mentioned above, trauma studies teach us that traumatic events create effects that last much longer than the time
of their occurrence. Consider two features of PTSD symptoms
in particular. First are emotional numbing and cognitive shut-
down. Much of the literature on trauma survivors describes
this dimension of trauma by talking about the absolute silence
that sits at the heart of traumatic experience. When we are
overwhelmed, what fails us most profoundly is our capacity
to use language, to make sounds that communicate meaning
from one person to another. I find myself still haunted by such
silence when it relates to 9/11. Second, there is the compulsion
to repeat the violence. For trauma survivors, it is as if the mind
becomes stuck in a playback loop. The mind keeps going over
the scene of violence, again and again, often unconsciously, in
an attempt to process it, but it is not able to do so. The mind's
meaning-making structures have collapsed, so it simply repeats
and recycles. Freud describes this compulsion to repeat not only
as an abstract image but also as a drive that shapes present-day
experience. "A patient," he states, "often feels strangely obliged
to repeat [the repressed material], the event as contemporary
experience, instead of remembering it as something that happened in the past."[1]

A neurobiologist friend of mine has given me a helpful, more physiological image. In the normal course of things, the information that we receive in experience goes through a time-stamping machine that marks it for storage in the appropriate part of the brain. When a traumatic experience occurs, the information rushes in too fast and furiously to be marked: it leaps over the time-stamper and, because it cannot be processed and stored, simply wanders and consistently replays itself. When this occurs, a person finds oneself, often inexplicably, reenacting the scene of violence, either in self-destructive actions (various forms of self-abuse) or in violent actions unleashed against others.

It is not hard to move from these descriptions of individual activity to an image of the collective national response to the events of 9/11. In my own mind, and in the minds of many, this scene of violence kept replaying itself. There was a literal replay: I saw the images over and over again—the planes flew in . . . the World Trade Center collapsed—I could not get the scene out of my head or off my TV screen. And then it eventually modulated to a different key and played on the radio and TV in the voice of George Bush. There was, it seemed to me, a collective desire to replay the scene and thereby incite the nation to violence in acting against the alleged perpetrators— or others who might serve as useful targets of recycled violence. And at the same time, we could not find the language to talk about what had happened to us. We were trapped in the silence of traumatic terror and the compulsion to relive it.

To quote Johannes Hofer again, trauma is a "disease due essentially to a disordered imagination."[2] To suffer from a traumatic stress disorder is to live in a mental world where the usual landmarks of meaning have fallen down. The most familiar path to reordering this disordered world is to repeat the event, but such repetition does not deal with the root cause: the memory that has nowhere to go. Is that not what followed 9/11, for the nation and the church, a disordering of our collective imaginations? And a compulsion to repeat it?

THE CHURCH'S WITNESS

Against the backdrop of this brief overview of what trauma theorists tell us about collective trauma and how we might experience it today, let me now ask: As we try to make meaning in the aftermath of collectively experienced traumatic events, what should be the work of the church? What are we to do as pastors and committed laypeople who seek to live and speak the gospel in the immediate and long-term aftermath of an eruption of violence such as 9/11?

Let me try one answer to that difficult question: *The church is called, as it exists in this space of trauma, to engage in the crucial task of reordering the collective imagination of its people and to be wise and passionate in this task.* As people of faith, the church enables us to be storytellers, weavers, artists, poets, and visionaries who take the repetitive violence of 9/11 and reframe it in the context of the story of our faith. We are called to help write the scripts of the Christian imagination as it seeks to bring order to this disorder, and we must do so in a manner that seeks the flourishing of all people.

To those of us from liberal Protestant church traditions, taking up this task of "telling stories" and "recrafting imagination" in a time of trauma may seem both too much and too little to ask. It seems to be too much because, in many ways, the liberal Protestant church conceded its storytelling, meaning-making powers years ago, giving over its imaginative sway to science, to experts, to the rational certainty of modernity. And it seems to be too little because as good Christian activists, we are trained to want action, to step into the streets and get things done. In this context, telling the story of faith seems too passive, too aesthetic and remote, an extravagance for happier and simpler times. However, an understanding of trauma and particularly of collective trauma indicates that the greatest political struggle we face concerns the ordering of our collective imagination—the matter of how we tell the story of what happened on 9/11 and what continues to happen in North America and around the

world. The imagination that is born out of this collective wrestling has and will continue to determine, profoundly, the future
course of our actions, both domestically and internationally;
and so the churches, as distinctive and strong Christian voices,
must be heard clearly in this struggle for imaginative space.

Having offered this image of people of faith as poets of the
imagination, I turn now to trauma-studies material to address
the issue of recovery and healing. What happens to the imagination as it struggles to move through experiences of traumatic violence? How does it begin to move out of the dissociated playback
loop where violence is reenacted again and again? At the heart
of the clinical material on recovery are three insights about this
process, insights useful for the theological-imaginative task.

*First, the person or persons who have experienced trauma need
to be able to tell their story.* The event needs to be spoken, pulled
out of the shadows of the mind into the light of day. When
we take this insight into a collective register, it means that as a
community, we need to give testimony. The truth of the violence, in its full scope, must be articulated.

*Second, there needs to be someone to witness this testimony, a
third-party presence that not only creates the safe space for speaking but also receives the words when they finally are spoken.* Collectively, as a church, we need to be willing to look hard at
the events unfolding around us, see them honestly, and receive
them fully.

*Third, the testifier and the witness (and we are both) must
begin the process of telling a new, different story together: we
must begin to pave a new road through the brain.* This third
requirement for recovery is an extremely tricky business. It
does not mean forgetting the past; rather, it means renarrating
the events in such a way that agency is returned and hope (a
future) is possible. All of this is aimed at breaking the cycle of
repetitive violence. Thus John, a Vietnam veteran, says that
recovery concerns the "socially re-constitutive act of storytelling" in which "we change the order of the way things are and
work towards preventing the enactment of similar horrors in
the future."[3] Maya Angelou speaks powerfully of the historical

significance of such retelling: "History, despite its wrenching pain, cannot be unlived; but if faced with courage, it need not be lived again."[4]

To translate these three insights about recovery and healing into the language of theology, as the church, we are called to be those who testify, who try to tell the story of what happened in its fullness; those who witness, who receive the story of violence and create a safe space for its healing; those who reimage the future by telling yet again—without denying the event of violence now woven into it—the story of our faith.

THREE FRAMING TALES

It may sound trite to call this speaking, listening, and retelling a difficult task. In the wake of 9/11, many different voices were seeking to frame the drama of violence that had just exploded upon us. In the week after the attacks, an article on the entertainment industry in the *New York Times* predicted three ways in which the dominant culture would seek to pursue its own task of storytelling, of reordering the collective imagination. The article described three kinds of movies and television programs that the industry did indeed subsequently promote: shows espousing family values, neighborly compassion, and the drama of personal sacrifice; stories about patriotism, celebrating the victory of democracy and the promise of global capitalism; and escapist comedies. To use Hofer's image, these story lines—family values, patriotism, and the distraction of comedy—were designed to be roads *through the brain of the nation,* roads carved out and constantly widening as the forces of industry pressed them insistently upon us.[5]

As persons of faith, it would be too easy for us to approach these stories with an attitude of simple dismissal. Each one of them has something important to say to us. Parts of them overlap with and illuminate the story Christians might tell to make sense of this event. But at crucial moments, these stories part ways with the Christian story. The stories of compassion

and family values were given to us vividly in news accounts of
the sacrifices human beings made for one another in the early
hours after the attack and the weeks and months that followed.
These were surely acts of courage that, when read in the context of the Christian story, deserved to be lifted up, witnessed,
and positively valued. Yet when told in our churches, these stories needed to be told with compassion and extended further
to include Arab and Muslim sisters and brothers who suddenly
feared for their lives in the United States and abroad. The story
of compassion and neighborly sacrifice needed then and needs
now to include accounts of families like that of the nine-year-
old Palestinian girl who was killed by Israeli troops at the same
time the World Trade Center was collapsing. We need to feel
culpable for our own history of violence. We need to remember, for instance, that Afghanistan, the possible origin of these
attacks, is presently considered the eleventh poorest country in
the world; its networks of familial relations are surely in a state
of utter disarray and shock from years of war and entrenched
poverty. In short, our stories of compassion must embrace the
suffering not only of our own wounded citizens and nation
when tragedy strikes, but of other beleaguered individuals and
countries as well. Otherwise, we tell a story of exclusionary
compassion inconsistent with the all-embracing love of God
that undergirds our faith.

The patriotic stories also have a place in our reordering of
the collective imagination. Indeed, many of the values that our
nation holds dear have deep resonance in the world of Scripture: an assertion of the basic integrity of each human person,
a call to create a world where justice abounds because universal
laws of love are followed, and a commitment to resist the power
of sin by dispersing power widely—a rough sketch of democracy. When these values are threatened, we need to stand up for
them and try to stop those who threaten them. But the rhetoric of the Bush White House and Pentagon moved decisively
toward a disturbingly different kind of patriotism, toward a plot
outline of revenge and retribution against an enemy who hides
in dark shadows. With these words, we saw the beginning of a

White House story line that laid the groundwork for aggressive military action, which caused many more people to suffer in actions that repeated a playback loop of violence. Arguably, we can view the appalling images of Abu Ghraib and Guantanamo as the products of the patriotic narrative articulated into new violence by the Bush administration. To use an earlier image, this story only carved more deeply into our imaginations a road of meaning-making that could not help but constantly reenact the scene of devastation rather than interrupt and transform it.

Consider also the third story line, the escapist comedy, perhaps the most dangerous of the three. What does it tell us about our nation's imagination and the Christian response we needed following 9/11 and continue to need today? The first thing to be said is that in the midst of events of trauma, we collectively need the release and the rejuvenation of laughter; we need ways to take in and celebrate the ongoing gifts of life and the goofy joy that attends us as we make our way through the messy world of human fellowship. But the comedy proposed by the dominant culture too often travels down the path of violent repetition and does so by offering the victim an easy way out of dealing with the root problem. In our culture, this is the way of a modern consumerist society, which seeks to respond to the complex challenges of grief, anger, and mourning by offering the escape of shallow pleasures, the escape of laughter born of compulsive consumption, and not by offering an honest look at the often comic and pleasurable indeterminacy of the human condition. In the week after the attacks, we saw our culture's determination to get on with this story of consumptive pleasure as we watched frantic workers in New York trying to feed electricity into the stock exchange through two hundred miles of fiber optic cables. When the work was completed, Wall Street paused for two reverent minutes and then began anew its mad scramble to buy and sell commodities, many of which serve no useful social function other than the production of the escapist pleasures on which we have learned to rely.

In Marxist language, this obsession is called commodity fetishism. In the language of today's world, it wears the name of Nike, Coca-Cola, GE, and GM. Like the escapist comedies we are certain to see, these commodities promise us fun and distracting delight. But such escapism blinds us to the destructive features of global capitalism, which create such enormous margins between those who have far too much and those with hardly anything at all. Although it is hard to see in the midst of pain and grief, we must learn to witness to the ways our own lifestyles, supported by the structures of global capitalism, contribute to a world where horrendous violence seems necessary and plausible to some people. Such escapism also distracts our battered minds and allows the memories and effects of violence to continue their reckless, brutal wanderings through our imaginations. Repetitive violence is allowed to deepen and widen its path through our collective imagination when we numb our minds with facile distractions.

CHURCH STORIES: A SYSTEMATIC THEOLOGICAL RESPONSE

Each of these stories, these cultural products, has been competing with the church to reorder our imaginations to their advantage. In response to these ongoing collective narratives of exclusionary compassion, vengeful patriotism, and escapist consumerism, what are the stories that we might tell in our churches? We could just uncritically concede the power of storytelling to the dominant media. But we have strong, compelling resources for doing otherwise.

As a systematic theologian, I argue that we might take up this task by turning to the stories of classical Christian doctrines and mining their resources for an alternative account of the events we witnessed on 9/11. Let me offer a hypothetical sketch of what such a journey might look like. I would begin my story with theological anthropology and discuss the long-standing traditions in Christian thought that assert the universal value of human beings—in all their magnificent and sometimes painful difference—as beloved creatures of God. In good systematic fashion, I would then move to an exploration of classical themes in the doctrine of sin; here I would discuss with you theological insights into the nature of original sin and the Christian insistence that, as God's beloved creatures, we are caught in webs of systemic evil that distort our capacities for good and destroy our powers to see the harms that hold us in their grip. I would discuss as well how this doctrine bids us to reflect, collectively, on the mutually implicating character of this sin, how together as nations and peoples we must critically assess the global webs of relations that brought us to 9/11. At the same time, I would remind us that even as we explore the systematic nature of sin, we cannot lose sight of individual responsibility for harms done and goods left undone.

From here, I would start to talk of grace. I would recall the doctrines of justification and sanctification and the truth they insist upon: that in the very moment we are marked as sinful by the world, God marks us as loved, as recipients of divine forgiveness. Marked in this way, we are freed to act not as perfect creatures, but as fallen people who are nonetheless called to persistently seek ways to embody God's will for the flourishing of all creation. Building on this hopeful image of ourselves, we could explore what it means for the church to be justified and sanctified in this same manner: how we become a community in the world that understands and witnesses to the depth of divine love for all people, solid in its testimony to the nature of God's righteousness, and at the same time profoundly open to and affected by the complex and often tragic nature of human actions.

I would bring us then into the stories and images of eschatology, of the Christian vision of the world as it should be and the resilient texture of hope born of faith. Here I would remind us that we come from a tradition that insists—vigorously insists—that as people of faith we must be courageously adept at living into the paradoxes that structure Christian existence, paradoxes like our call to hold together, in times like these, a sense of tragic realism and utopian expectation. Paradoxes teaching us that we must live in the tension of knowing that we are deeply responsible moral agents and yet that the ultimate claim upon us is God's, who seeks fellowship with us even in the midst of our fallen moral actions, and who gives us the grace to act in the first place.

All of these doctrinal stories position us not to seek easy answers when we look at scenes of violence such as video clips of the planes crashing into buildings on 9/11. Rather, they teach us to seek to understand ever anew how sin and grace exist together in the complex matrix of violence. With this understanding we must ask what it means to be faithful in a world perched on the edge of a new and seemingly ever more violent millennium.

I have just told you how, if I were to don the garb of the systematic theologian, I might frame the task of reconstructing our collective imagination. But another alternative is at hand that is perhaps even more powerful for the Christian church. Instead of developing the doctrinal outline I have sketched above, I would suggest that the immediacy of storytelling and its resources for imaginatively crafting the world around us is at hand in the Bible. Accordingly, I return here to the story with which I began, the tale of the disciples meeting Jesus on the road to Emmaus.

SCRIPTURE AND THE REORDERED IMAGINATION

At the beginning of the story, we meet two disciples who are walking along a well-carved-out road and, as Luke tells us, are talking. Might we imagine that they are talking rather frantically, talking fast and at times confusedly? A barely suppressed hysteria registers in their voices; their leader has just been tortured and executed, and they are trying to make sense of it, trying to reorder their disordered thoughts. In the process, they are probably replaying the scene of the crucifixion again and again. As they recall—or perhaps they cannot remember—the violent events that happened just days before, they seem to be stuck in a playback loop, having lost both their hope and their future. These disciples, these disoriented witnesses to a devastating event, are trauma survivors. Even though they were not themselves tortured and nailed to a cross, they bear in their speech and their bodies the reality of the horror that unfolded before them and forever pulled their lives into its drama. As they walk along and talk about it, they perhaps are, in their own way, struggling to testify to and be faithful witnesses of the trauma that holds them in its powerful grip. Might we imagine as well that the first-century equivalent of video clips course through their imaginations as they wrestle with the stories that the dominant culture is telling about what happened?

Then, out of nowhere, Jesus walks up and joins them; but they are too disordered to see him. He walks along with them, in their trauma, in silence, listening to the gaping hole that sits at the middle of their crazed speech. Notice that it is Jesus who comes to them. The disciples, in their pain and fear, do not have to figure out how to reach him. He simply appears, full-bodied and present. Here, then, is God coming to us, even in this moment of violence as we babble in fear. This coming of God into the place of disordering violence is crucial to our understanding of the events around us; as clergy, could it be that our call is primarily to announce God's already-enacted advent, the divine coming? If so, then we need to remember that as we seek to minister in a world too full of violence, we do not need to make God appear, for God is here already. Our task is to proclaim God's presence.

When Jesus finally speaks in the passage, he decisively intervenes in the story the disciples have just told him about the events they have witnessed. Interrupting their frantic speech, he calls the disciples "foolish." This suggests that God knows how we will tell distorted stories of our traumatic events, stories that perpetuate further harm, stories that bear in them marks of the violence that haunt us. Jesus steps into the playback loop that holds their imaginations, and he speaks. What does Jesus do when he breaks their pattern of storytelling? Remarkably, he begins to reconstruct their account of his death and continued life, and he does so by first interpreting for them the tale of

"Moses and the prophets." He reorders the disciples' imagination by pulling it into the history of God's relation with Israel.
Even when he does this, however, they still do not recognize
him. Their dissociated conversation continues, as does ours.

Nevertheless, Luke tells us that the disciples find this strange
teacher interesting and so invite him for dinner. Jesus initially
appears to be "going on" ahead, but the day is "far spent" (KJV).
Darkness is falling. Perhaps the well-carved road to Emmaus is
getting hard to see. So he agrees to stay with them, and they
gather for a meal. We hear that Jesus takes bread and blesses
and breaks it and gives it to them. In this simple ritual action,
memory is sparked—a lost truth recalled—and suddenly their
eyes are opened, and they recognize him. Jesus is finally made
known to them in an event of life-giving communion. In this
moment, we find the reality of grace breaking into their midst
not through an act of exclusionary compassion, but rather
through a bodily gesture that is deeply embracing. This is no
escapist meal of commodified junk food, a gathering of surface
pleasures; it is a meal that nourishes and strengthens, and most
important, it is a meal that opens their eyes. They see differently. The repetitive cycle is broken, and their imaginations are
reframed around a shared table, not set to celebrate a vengeful
patriotic victory, but a table of healing and fellowship.

Here the story takes another sudden turn: Jesus vanishes at
the very instant they see him, and the disciples fall into disbelief again. They know they have seen the risen Lord, and they
excitedly return to Jerusalem to tell their friends. One can feel
their sense of urgency as they struggle, back at home, to testify
to God's presence among them on the road, to be witnesses to
the good news of new life. But they still fail to truthfully see
him when he comes to them once again, now in their home
place. As the story continues, the reader witnesses the disciples
wrestling with the ongoing effects of traumatic violence upon
them. They want to believe in a world where Jesus lives, where
hope flourishes, but they cannot seem to get there. They say
all the right words, but the truth remains elusive. Recognition
comes in waves. Belief and horror stand together.

According to Lawrence Langer, after trauma we never return to a state of previous innocence. "The survivor does not travel a road from the normal to the bizarre [and] back to the normal again, . . . but from the normal to the bizarre [and] back to a normalcy so permeated by the bizarre encounter with atrocity that it can never be purified again. The two worlds haunt each other."[6] The Scripture offers us a similar warning: the way forward is not through a naive forgetting or escapist comedy. Whatever grace we see—and seek to proclaim—will and should be a grace haunted by the ghost of the violence it addresses.

This haunted reality is displayed in the final words of the story that Luke tells us. The disciples have their most powerful experience of seeing Jesus when he shows them the wounds in his hands and feet: the way forward will be into the heart of the wounds. By being receptive to grace that continually vanishes and returns, we learn that it will come when we are ready, as a church, to look soberly and straightforwardly at the wounds of the world that produced 9/11 and not fall prey to the dazzling power of a Hollywood story line. This state of haunted truth-telling is the place we must stand to remember the horrors of 9/11 and their aftermath. We must not give way to aggression and the repetitive cycle of violence if we are to move into the third step of recovery described earlier, where we can imagine a healing story and a hopeful future.

While the disciples are still wondering at these things, Jesus gives them fish to eat: the way forward will emerge most clearly when bodies are fed and rest is offered, when the superficial joy born of commodity fetishism is replaced by real feeding and care of all who are hungry and ill.

Finally, Jesus says, "Peace be with you." That such words could come from so broken a body is truly a wonder, and it is a word of hope for us especially when we are wounded. Imagine, if you will, the video of the terrorist attacks being played in a church service where it is surrounded by the liturgy, Scripture, theology, hymns, and prayers of a community that has truly ingested the words of Jesus in all their astute simplicity: "Peace be with you."

Imagine now that we pull back, leave church, and remember the smoky skyline of New York, the plane wreckage in Pennsylvania, the crumbled Pentagon, the barrios on the Texas border, the struggling peasants in Chiapas, the rubble within and around Jerusalem, the Palestinian family eating dinner, a small and isolated and poor village in the mountains of Afghanistan, a child pulling on her mother's veil. . . . This panoramic video is the world that God sees—and has walked into and offered fish to share with us. His silence holds our trauma. His rebuke bids us to think critically. His story of Moses pulls us into a long history of trauma and hope. His words, "Peace be with you," give us a vision of what we are called to create among ourselves now and in the days to come.

The Bush administration unquestionably pursued a path of violence in response to the trauma of 9/11. Still, I continue to imagine powerful theological resources to counter this story of revenge; it is not the only narrative available to our collective imaginations. Actually, although we may not always be able to easily access peace or straightforwardly surrender to its life-giving potential, the peace we seek often lies within us. We will find it already in the recesses of our imaginations and the deeply held stories we tell about the real meaning of these lives we lead, this world that we love, these roads that we walk, and perhaps most important, the lessons we learn from the strangers that we meet.

3

Soul Anatomy

The Healing Acts of Calvin's Psalms

When I speak to churches and community groups about religion and violence, they are rarely prepared for me to bring up the name John Calvin.[1] Though he is the founder of Reformed Protestant theology, many people, even in Reformed churches, have no idea who he was. And those who are familiar with his legacy often associate it with rigid doctrines and Swiss repressive theocracy. Yet Calvin, I argue, offers profound wisdom regarding the way in which grace meets violence—wisdom that is strikingly relevant in today's world. The following essay turns to Calvin's most famous biblical commentary, a reading of Psalms, to explore the theological relation of grace and violence. Calvin called the book an "anatomy of all parts of the soul," thereby meaning it was a map of a human soul, divided, torn, haunted, rageful, terrorized, and yet amazingly made ever hopeful through the enduring presence of grace awakened in prayer.

A tragic pastoral experience first catapulted me into Calvin's Psalms commentary. For many years I worshiped in a small UCC (United Church of Christ) congregation in downtown New Haven, Connecticut; several years ago we experienced a terrible event in our community. Latisha, a fourteen-year-old congregant, was walking home from school one afternoon when she unexpectedly witnessed a drive-by shooting in which a young man died. Because she was the only eyewitness, she not only had to deal with the traumatic aftershock of seeing it happen before her eyes; she also agreed to testify about it in court, which required reliving the moment again and again before a judge and eventually a jury. Latisha's mother was not well through much of the ordeal; in her absence, a small group of women deacons committed themselves to taking Latisha to therapy sessions, sitting with her in the courthouse, and most important, listening to her as she talked about not just the original event but also the ongoing trauma of rehearsing it on the witness stand.

As one might imagine, the shock of such an event is hard, and when it falls on a girl on the edge of adulthood, its effects are dramatically apparent. She manifested all the classic symptoms of traumatic shock and did so with teenage intensity. Although Latisha was, like most fourteen-year-olds, not much of a Bible reader, the women supporting her were, and they turned to the Psalms for solace and guidance as they walked with her. In the midst of their well-orchestrated, support-group-style Bible study, they asked me to provide a scholarly interpretation of these much-beloved poems. They thought it might help.

I brought them Calvin's *Commentary on the Psalms*, a book I had never read before but was eager to explore, particularly given this pastorally intense occasion. Over the years, I have found that my most productive "scholarly" readings of Calvin have often been birthed not in the library stacks but in rooms filled with women trying to figure out how to cope with life's daily challenges. What unfolded in those sessions this time was true to my previous experience: our shared interpretation was not just illuminating; it was brilliant—in the truest sense of the word. A bright light was thrown upon Latisha and upon our experience of trying to walk beside her in a way that felt respectful, faithful, and hope-filled. As we read, Calvin worked through the psalms, one by one, and as we followed along in our own reading of Psalms, we enacted a collective, ritual healing that in uncanny ways paralleled what I knew from contemporary trauma theory about the processes by which people heal from violence. It was as if Calvin, along with King David or another psalmist, was speaking to us in the present moment: alive, engaged, and powerfully pastoral. And the whole group of us—Calvin, David, Serene, Latisha, and her Bible-reading caregivers—made our way forward in ways as surprising as they were wise.

THE LEGACY OF JOHN CALVIN

To understand the power of this witness, some general background information on Calvin's life and work is useful. He is most famous for his work *The Institutes of the Christian Religion*, a text he revised over and again throughout his life, a compendium of Christian doctrine.[2] Beginning students of Reformed theology often overlook Calvin's prolific nature: he wrote volumes of tracts, lectures, letters, sermons, and most important, a series of biblical commentaries. The importance of commentaries is signaled in the preface to the *Institutes*, where Calvin explains that his major doctrinal work is first and foremost a tool designed to help students read the Bible. This fact has led theologians interested in Calvin's work to take very seriously the volumes he devoted directly to scriptural exegesis and reflection. In volumes such as the *Commentary on the Book of Psalms*,[3] Calvin gives us his *firsthand* encounter with the Word of God, which stands at the foundation of Reformed theology. When we explore his commentaries, we are digging into the bedrock of his thought.

In the pages of this text, we see Calvin at his theological best as he grapples conceptually with issues like predestination, providence, suffering, Christology, and the character of God's sovereignty. We meet a theologian who is not afraid to jump into the messiness of everyday life and explain how this poetry might help one negotiate difficult everyday issues and challenges. When he approached the Bible, he did not see before him a set of simplistic propositional claims from which

the mainstream religion of his day. Like David, he also found himself in a world divided into (at least in his mind) two sets of persons: the faithful who are being unjustly assaulted by "the evil ones," and the evil perpetrators who forcefully seek to do harm to the faithful.[7] And like David, Calvin's communal commitment pushed him not just to take sides but also to stand up publicly to the rulers of his day and to argue for justice and freedom for his people.[8]

Calvin's own experience of persecution meant that, like David, he was also quite aware of the distinct pastoral needs of his community. He knew from the inside that their pain was not what one suffers in the wake of disease or lost love or the torture of a guilty conscience; rather, it was the pain one wrestles with when someone actively and aggressively seeks to *harm you*—and bewildered and angered by it, you are rendered helpless in the face of it. He describes this state of excruciating pain as "terrorized conscience" and as living in a world marked by "mental distress" and "protracted sorrow," a world where it seems as if "hell opened to receive them."[9] It is the suffering of those for whom faith has lost its meaning because all they know, day in and day out, is the violent attacks of an enemy they cannot escape, and the horror of watching those they love cut down before their eyes. Helpless and rage-filled, they watch their own lives devolve into sorrow, grief, and a rapidly dissolving zeal for living. Like the folks of old to whom the Psalms were written, they embodied the anatomy of a tortured soul.

Contrary to most popular readings of Calvin that interpret his "terrorized conscience" as referring to an internal, deep-seated, personally produced "furnace of sin" that leads us to sin constantly against God and our neighbors—in this book Calvin assumes that "terror of mind" is provoked by external persecution. This particular form of terror does not spring from a roiling inner reservoir of inborn sin; it is produced by violence done *to* them, not *by* them. By focusing on the mental distress caused by this violence, Calvin also makes it clear that he wants to help his readers cope not just with the physical effects of violence, but also with its deeply emotional effects as well. He

tries to address the complex weave of feelings and psychic agonies that haunted them, as well as the more obviously rational,
ideational questions raised for them by their suffering. He is
similarly aware that their suffering is *ongoing* (not just a past
event), that it is *collective* (not just individual and personal),
and that it involves their social isolation and marginalization:
they are persons whose meaning systems exist outside the dominant systems of meaning in which they find themselves both
within France and as refugees from France.[10]

All this is to say that when Calvin stepped into the world
of Scripture via the Psalms, he stepped into a world conso-
nant with his own: a world that collective social violence had
knocked out of kilter. Using his theological and rhetorical
genius, he interpreted the Psalms in a manner that invited his
suffering readers into plays of mind and vistas of faithful imagination that he believed would offer them hope and healing.[11]
To do this, he undertakes a strange and haunting journey deep
into the heart of suffering. He engages in the art of theological
soul-craft, to offer his readers a set of "imaginative practices"
(stage scripts) designed to help them cope—visions crafted to
strengthen them, and most crucially, to make grace alive for
them as they dwell in this terrifying space. And here is where
trauma theory becomes, for us, an interesting conversation
partner.

CALVIN, TRAUMA THEORY, AND THE
COMMENTARY—AN ANATOMY OF THE SOUL

By focusing on this "traumatic" dimension of Calvin's enterprise, I do not imply that we might best understand the
Commentary on Psalms by haphazardly applying to it the contemporary psychological categories used by trauma theorists.
Rather, I want to suggest something methodologically much
looser: when we read Calvin's writings with the Bible in one
hand and the work of trauma theorists in the other, we are
able to identify certain resonant patterns of meaning that

might otherwise not come to the foreground of our theological reflections. At the center of these resonant patterns is Calvin's remarkable capacity to enter the violence-torn world of his readers' imagination and to speak, in this space, a theologically powerful—and timeless—word of hope and healing, or to use Calvin's words, to render for us an anatomy of the soul.

The field of trauma studies is rich with insights that help illumine this claim, the most profound of which, for me, is the growing awareness that such violence creates in human beings a kind of cognitive breakdown that is as much neurological and physical as it is emotional and intellectual. To use a phrase often invoked by trauma theorists, traumatized people are "undone selves." Judith Herman, an important theorist in the field whose work I touched on briefly in the first chapter, summarizes these complex dynamics in the following manner:

> Traumatized people feel utterly abandoned, utterly alone, cast out of the human and divine systems of care and protection that sustain life. Thereafter, a sense of alienation, of disconnection, pervades every relationship, from the most intimate familial bonds to the most abstract affiliations of community and religion. When trust is lost, traumatized people feel that they belong more to the dead than to the living.[12]

In a remarkable passage in which Calvin reflects on the lament of Psalm 88, Calvin uses strikingly similar language to describe what his persecuted readers and the lamenting psalmist must have been experiencing in the midst of their traumatic suffering. After using verse 5 of the psalm to depict them as living a state in which one feels "free among the dead, like the slain who lie in the grave, whom thou rememberest no more, and who are cut off from thy hand," Calvin offers his own interpretation of this particular plight. He tells us that the psalmist stands "with those who have been wounded, [as] he bewails his condition as worse than if, enfeebled by calamities, he were going down to death by little and little; for we are naturally inspired with horror at the prospect of a violent death."[13] What more powerful testimony could one give to the reality described by Herman than this?

In his description of the overarching purpose of the Psalms, Calvin offers an account of the Scripture as a text in which conflicting and often incoherent feelings and thoughts can be given over to speech:

> I have been accustomed to call this book, I think not inappropriately, "an Anatomy of All Parts of the Soul," for there is not an emotion of which any one can be conscious that is not here represented as in a mirror. Or rather, the Holy Spirit has here drawn to the life of all the griefs, sorrows, fears, doubts, hopes, cares, perplexities, in short, all the distracting emotions with which the minds of men are wont to be agitated. The other parts of Scripture contain the commandments that God enjoined his servants to announce to us. But here [in the Psalms] the prophets themselves, seeing they are exhibited to us as speaking to God, and laying open all their inmost thoughts and affections, call, or rather draw, each of us to the examination of himself in particular, in order that none of the many infirmities to which we are subject, and of the many vices with which we abound, may remain concealed. It is certainly a rare and singular advantage, when all lurking places are discovered, and the heart is brought into the light, purged from that most baneful infection, hypocrisy.[14]

Bringing to light sorrows and fears hidden away in "lurking places." Speaking the unspeakable. Giving language to a heart whose pain has made it speechless. This is what Calvin describes as the rare power of the psalmist. Thus the psalmist expresses the agonies of those whose innermost emotional world has become the source of their deepest infirmity. Calvin makes this point later in the commentary, using the words of another teacher of the church to describe what the psalmist accomplishes in speech. He tells us that the Davidic poet offers up the "kind of complaint [which] justly deserves to be reckoned among the unutterable groaning of which Paul makes mention."[15]

But understanding the plight of the traumatized, describing the feelings and dispositions created by traumatic experience, is not enough for either Calvin or trauma theorists. For Calvin, articulating unutterable groans is only a part of the theological work undertaken in the Psalms. To provide a full "anatomy of all parts of the soul," people must not only outwardly speak about the violence they have seen and felt; they must also open themselves to the healing power of grace in their lives. For Calvin, this means accepting the promise that God has made to be ever present to them in their suffering and, in being present, to redeem and transform their plight as they stand "groaning" before the Divine.

As to how this transformation happens, Calvin offers no trivial answer, no easy fixes, and no abstract platitudes. Like the psalmist, he refuses to blithely tell readers that their faith will carry them through hard times if they just believe strongly enough, or that God has preordained their persecution and they should therefore endure it patiently. Even more important, he does not glorify their suffering or suggest that their mental anguish is a test designed by God to measure the depth of their piety. Rather, he enters into the depths of their traumatic anguish: instead of explaining *why* they are suffering, he offers them a concrete "practice" to hold their suffering. He lays before them a collective pattern of thinking, acting, and feeling that he believes has the power to soothe their mental distress even as they continue to experience the ravaging force of traumatic events. The practice—the stage script—he offers is deceptively simple; it is the practice undertaken by the psalmist himself: prayer.

THE HEALING PERFORMANCE OF PRAYER: WE TESTIFY, GOD WITNESSES

In a section that immediately follows his description of the Psalms as "an anatomy of all parts of the soul" (the section quoted above), Calvin explains to his readers why prayer holds such promise for their healing.

In short, as calling upon God is one of the principal means of securing our safety, and as a better and more unerring rule for guiding us in this exercise cannot be elsewhere than in the Psalms, it follows, that in proportion to the proficiency which a man shall have attained in understanding them, will be his knowledge of the most important part of celestial doctrine. Genuine and earnest prayer proceeds first from a sense of our need, and next, from faith in the promises of God. It is by perusing these inspired compositions [the Psalms], that men will be most effectually awakened to a sense of their maladies, and, at the same time, instructed in seeking remedies for their cure. In a word, whatever may serve to encourage us when we are about to pray to God, is taught us in this book.[16]

The entire body of Calvin's commentary is devoted to showing his readers how this transformation of imagination happens when we lift up our groaning to the Divine. And by showing his readers the dispositions that psalmlike prayer evokes in its practitioners, Calvin tries to inculcate in his readers the actual practice/disposition he is describing. Through the play of his own rhetoric, in other words, he pragmatically demonstrates the discursive mechanism by which prayer, as the paradigmatic Christian practice, reconfigures the experience of trauma itself.

Although contemporary scholars in the field of trauma studies acknowledge that there are myriad ways in which persons learn to survive and, at times, even flourish in the aftermath of traumatic violence, there is general consensus that healing unfolds—at the very least—as a three-staged process. Judith Herman describes this process as follows: "The central task of the first stage is the establishment of safety. The central task of the second stage is remembrance and mourning. The central task of the third stage is reconnection with ordinary life."[17] She and others also argue that as this process unfolds, there needs to be an ongoing, dynamic conversation taking place between a testifier and a witness—between the survivor who offers testimony to the harm endured and the person who, having helped to establish a sense of safety for the survivor, witnesses the traumatic speech.[18]

In testifying, the survivor gives voice to previously unspeakable agony, and in witnessing, the receiver of the testimony is able to confirm that the survivor's voice is heard and that the plight no longer needs to be hidden in a dark corner of the soul, but can be pulled into the light of day and affirmed as a reality worthy of sustained lamentation and possible redress. As this reciprocal play of speaking and hearing unfolds, the two conversation partners together begin to undertake the task of writing a story about the trauma that allows it, in the long run, to be integrated into a broader and more expansive story of hope and hence of future possibilities for fullness of life.

It is striking that throughout the commentary, Calvin uses the language of testifying and witnessing to describe what happens when a person turns to God in prayer. When one dares to lift up to God the most painful and often unseemly torments of one's soul, one testifies to God—one tells the Divine directly—the story of one's deepest affections and emotions, including the depths of pain suffered. In prayer, one tells God the tale of one's trauma, a tale that is often impossible to tell, at least initially, in the language of everyday experience. Calvin also refers to God as the one who "witnesses" this story, in all its messy and inarticulate indeterminacy. For example, in his reading of Psalm 10:13, Calvin states forthrightly that God is "the witness of all our affections."[19] When we pray, God is the one who receives our speaking and, in so doing, affirms the reality of our suffering.

Calvin further insists that when this dynamic of testifying and witnessing transpires in prayer, a person's own story undergoes a transformation as it is pulled into and redefined by the divine story of God's constant presence with us, and God's promise to ultimately redeem the harm done to us and thus make "all things right." In this way, the practice of prayer allows our broken speech to be knit together in the space of divine speech. Likewise, it allows for our experiences of isolation and hopelessness to be recast in the space of divine grace, recast as experiences in which we are not alone but rather exist with a God who offers us, unceasingly, a future.

THE THREE STAGES OF PSALMIC HEALING

The similarities between trauma studies and Calvin's theology become even more apparent when we compare Herman's account of the three stages of healing with Calvin's standard division of the Psalms into three basic types of prayers: psalms of deliverance, psalms of lamentation, and psalms of thanksgiving.[20] In his analysis of the three different functions of the Psalms, Calvin describes a mode of divine presence and human response that resonates with Herman's tripartite typology of recovery from trauma.

Stage One: Psalms of Deliverance: Establishing Safety, Providence, and Divine Witnessing

Psalm 10:12–18

> [12]Rise up, O Lord; O God, lift up your hand;
>   do not forget the oppressed.
> [13]Why do the wicked renounce God,
>   and say in their hearts, "You will not call us to
>   account"?
> [14]But you do see! Indeed you note trouble and grief,
>   that you may take it into your hands;
>   the helpless commit themselves to you;
>   you have been the helper of the orphan.
> [15]Break the arm of the wicked and evildoers;
>   seek out their wickedness until you find none.
> [16]The Lord is king forever and ever;
>   the nations shall perish from his land.
> [17]O Lord, you will hear the desire of the meek;
>   you will strengthen their heart, you will incline your ear
> [18]to do justice for the orphan and the oppressed,
>   so that those from earth may strike terror no more.

In his exploration of the psalms of deliverance—such as Psalm 10—Calvin describes a form of praying in which a person directly asks God for support in and rescue from the calamities of life. In such prayers, the psalmist invokes the reality of a God who has the power and the compassion necessary to respond to such beseeching. When Calvin reads these psalms, he focuses on what they tell us about the sovereign power and merciful love of God. He repeatedly tells his readers that in the verses of these psalms, we clearly see that God desires to deliver us from the evil of those who assail us and that God has the power to ultimately do this because God is ruler of the universe in all its vast complexity and mystery. By emphasizing the goodness and righteous power of God, Calvin creates a theological framework designed to assure his readers that in the midst of their trauma, they are safe and can trust God.

Following the insights of Herman into the first stage of healing, it seems to me that this type of praying forms in its practitioner three habits of imagination crucial to the process of recovering from traumatic stress. First, it is crucial that Calvin invoke, at the beginning of his training in the art of prayer, the reality of God's sovereignty because this dimension of divine identity provides the traumatized with a profound sense of safety, which they so strongly lack as they wander in the world of the dead. Calvin makes this point when he stresses that if this God, the ultimate determiner and orderer of all, is actually in control of everything, then we can rest assured that the forces of violence assailing us will not, in the final analysis, determine our ultimate reality. For persons whose world has been knocked out of kilter by traumatic events, the invocation of divine control can serve to stabilize their seemingly unstable reality by bringing order into the midst of their experiences of profound disorder. With this stabilization comes the possibility of imagining that one is, in the most ultimate sense, safe. It becomes possible to imagine that the deepest truth about oneself is that God loves you. Such love creates a new sense of order and thus relativizes the disorder that violence created around you and within you.

Second, by stressing that we can earnestly "trust" this God who determines the ultimate order of things, Calvin not only stabilizes our discursive environment; he also shows that our environment becomes a place where we imagine our traumatic speech being actively received by a powerful, open, accepting, and witnessing God. Calvin thus evokes an imaginative space where the traumatized self experiences the protection of God's enveloping arms and receptive ear. In such a space, he suggests, we feel free to express those unutterable groans that violence has stifled in our souls. Prayers of deliverance provide a space where trust ushers repressed voices into speech, a space where those who feel isolated and silenced by the world find permission to unguardedly express their formerly inexpressible agony of spirit to a God who stands before them, seeing them, receiving their woes, witnessing their calming horror.

Out of this sense of safety and trust comes a third important disposition performed by the psalmist in his psalms of deliverance. By assuring readers that God is in control and that they are protected and heard by God, Calvin creates an imaginative space where those who have felt helplessness in the face of violence can once again imagine themselves as agents whose actions in the world matter. On the surface, it might seem counterintuitive that giving control of one's life over to God can have the inverse effect of increasing one's sense of personal agency and control, but the literature on trauma suggests otherwise. It proposes that trauma survivors desperately need to believe that the world is fundamentally ordered and trustworthy if they, in turn, are to have the capacity to imagine themselves as meaningful actors within it again. This enabling order can take many forms; parents, communities, nations, and myriad other institutions and persons can provide the contextual arena within which this can happen. What Calvin teaches in the psalms of deliverance is that the most

enduring way to establish this sense of human agency is in the
context of divine agency.

Stage Two: Psalms of Lament and Mourning: Remembering and Offering Testimony

Psalm 22

¹ My God, my God, why have you forsaken me?
    Why are you so far from helping me?

. . . .

¹²Many bulls encircle me,
    strong bulls of Bashan surround me;
¹³they open wide their mouths at me,
    like a ravening and roaring lion.
¹⁴I am poured out like water,
    and all my bones are out of joint;
    my heart is like wax;
    it is melted within my breast;
¹⁵my mouth is dried up like a potsherd,
    and my tongue sticks to my jaws;
    you lay me in the dust of death.
¹⁶For dogs are all around me;
    a company of evildoers encircles me.
    My hands and feet have shriveled.

. . . .

²⁰Deliver my soul from the sword,
    my life from the power of the dog!
²¹Save me from the mouth of the lion!

. . . .

²⁴For he did not despise or abhor
    the affliction of the afflicted;
    he did not hide his face from me,
    but heard when I cried to him.

In Calvin's discussion of prayers of lamentation, he moves
into a textual world where the sentiments invoked by the psalmist
resonate with Herman's description of the second stage of healing: remembrance and mourning. After trauma survivors begin

to speak, to trust, and to connect with others in the first stage, they then begin the more arduous process of actually speaking about the original traumatic events and their aftermath. They begin to remember and tell the stories of what happened to them and grieve the losses they have sustained. When this activity of remembering starts, the victim need not get all the facts correct. Often the events themselves cannot be "accurately" retrieved because in the original experience of violence, one's usual mechanisms of cognition and memory may have been disabled or overwhelmed by the magnitude of the event. When this occurs, the events do not mentally register. Hence, there is often no straightforward memory to excavate; there are only gaps, silences, and a vast range of emotions and vague, dreamlike images that move in and out of one's consciousness. To remember, in this context, is to give linguistic shape and substance to these silences, emotions, and dreams, to pull them out of the "lurking corners" Calvin describes, and to do so in a manner such that one "is effectually awakened to a sense of their maladies."[21]

In describing the psalms as "awakening us" to a sense of our "maladies," Calvin rightly discerns that in this activity of remembering, one is not engaged in a straightforward process of simply recollecting previously known subject matter. At this stage in the healing process, the act of speaking involves actively creating a new discursive awareness of something previously unknown. As Calvin often reminds his readers, it is only when they hear the psalmist lament the harm done to him that they, by mimicking his words as they pray, find a language for and an awareness of the trauma they have endured. As the trauma literature further tells us, it is important that these emerging sentiments not be negatively judged or criticized as inappropriate, false, immoral, or incoherent; they simply are what they are—the groans of the violated. Further, when the groans are heard, in all their incoherence and emotional volatility, the traumatized person begins to develop the capacity to mourn the harm done to them. Along with remembering comes the process of grieving—of deeply lamenting—the traumatic reality to which one is testifying.

When I first ventured into Calvin's analysis of the psalms of lamentation, the degree to which he encourages his readers to identify with the often-violent rage of the psalmist and to viciously hate the "wicked ones," meaning the dogs, the liars, the evildoers who have hurt them—this encouragement made me quite uncomfortable. In these psalms, Calvin fully shares the writer's sense that the world can be sharply divided into two groups of people, the good and the evil, and that the good people who have suffered the oppression of the evil ones have every right to want their oppressors to suffer, to be punished by God, to be annihilated by divine wrath. As he reads through these psalms, he refuses to remove the sharp edges of these feelings; actually, he often goes farther than the psalmist in expressing his anger, outrage, despair, urge for revenge, and desire for unspeakable harm to befall the wicked. In this respect, his account of these psalms is uncomfortably rough, assaultive, emotional, and rage-filled.

When I began to read these psalms in light of trauma literature, however, my assessment shifted; I was less troubled and more intrigued by the rhetorical force of Calvin's interpretation. I began to understand that by allowing the full range of human emotions to surface in his reading of these psalms, Calvin creates a vivid imaginative space within which his readers can similarly experience, without negative judgment, the outrage and grief that emerge as they remember and name the traumatic harm they have suffered. Moreover, I appreciated how these sentiments may have provided his readers with a language they might not initially have possessed but which they could now actively inhabit as they struggled to speak. I saw as well that demonizing their perpetrators was an essential part of their healing process, and that admitting the depth of their anger toward their persecutors was a necessary precursor to his community's return to the land of the living. Given this, Calvin's skills at vitriolic oration impressed me as a theological strength rather than as a discomforting theological weakness. I saw that perhaps the more caustic his language became, the more expansive the possibilities of healing.

Stage Three: Psalms of Thanksgiving: Reintegration of the Mundane and the Scope of Divine Grace

Psalm 119

[54]Your statutes have been my songs
    wherever I make my home.

. . . .

[103]How sweet are your words to my taste,
    sweeter than honey to my mouth!

. . . .

[129]Your decrees are wonderful;
    therefore my soul keeps them.
[130]The unfolding of your words gives light;
    it imparts understanding to the simple.

. . . .

[165]Great peace have those who love your law;
    nothing can make them stumble.
[166]I hope for your salvation, O Lord,
    and I fulfill your commandments.
[167]My soul keeps your decrees;
    I love them exceedingly.
[168]I keep your precepts and decrees,
    for all my ways are before you.

. . . .

[171]My lips will pour forth praise,
    because you teach me your statutes.
[172]My tongue will sing of your promise,
    for all your commandments are right.
[173]Let your hand be ready to help me,
    for I have chosen your precepts.
[174]I long for your salvation, O Lord,
    and your law is my delight.
[175]Let me live that I may praise you,
    and let your ordinances help me.

The angry prayers of lamentation are not the last word with which Calvin leaves his readers. He also devotes his attention to a third category, psalms of thanksgiving; among a wide range of topics, they include the poetic sensibility expressed in Psalm

119, as just one example. Like the two previous categories of psalms, his interpretation of this third category bears striking resemblance to Herman's third stage of healing: reconnection with everyday life. In this stage of healing the trauma survivor and the witness undertake together the task of telling a story in which the now-articulated experience of trauma is woven into an account of daily life. This requires telling a story in which the survivor's tale of the violence done is not forgotten or unrealistically glorified but is, rather, integrated into patterns of speech and forms of knowledge that are broader, more complex, and experientially more comprehensive than the disrupted discourse of trauma.

This third stage of healing often takes a lifetime to enact. It consists of things like learning how to remember the violent death of a friend and still enjoy tasks such as baking bread, caring for children, or attending a Sunday morning Psalm sing. To do this integrative work is difficult, not only at a practical level, but also and perhaps even more important, at the level of imagination. It requires having an interior world capable of managing images of both haunting violence and of kneading bread, each envisioned in its fullness as well as in its relativized relation to the other. It is only when one's imagination has been so capacitated, Herman suggests, that the trauma survivor can begin to hope and to act in personally empowering ways.

This integration unfolds for readers in Calvin's interpretations of the psalms of thanksgiving. Here Calvin not only shows readers how to render praise to God for their deliverance from the harm of grand enemies and vast nations; he also uses quite commonplace references to ground his descriptions of everyday, commonplace praiseworthy events. He refers to the splendor of nature as a hallmark of God's continued presence with us. Imagery of eating, feasting, resting, walking safely, sleeping peacefully, of life lived in a web of secure relations and hope—all these serve as reminders that the God whose providence protects us and whose witnessing ears and eyes receive us, is also a God who offers us a future. In that future, violence need no longer be the determinative reality of our imaginative landscapes because God gives us food, sleep, daily work, and the bonds of human community. Through these psalms, in other words, Calvin takes a world that has been thrown out of kilter and not only stabilizes it, but also weaves it back into a worldview where violence itself no longer determines the central features of one's ongoing experience.

What is also remarkable is how Calvin accomplished this reintegration into the mundane: not by pretending that the traumas never happened or will somehow magically disappear because they have been remembered and mourned, but rather by allowing the reality of violence testified to in the first two types of psalms to continue to echo through the praising prayers of this third type of psalm. He admits that praise itself must often emerge in the midst of continued suffering and persecution. What is crucial, therefore, is not to have the pain disappear or the forces of violence cease to bear down upon us, but to reduce the hold that traumatic violence has upon the imaginative capacity of the one who suffers. In these psalms, hope returns not because evil is explained or immediate justice is invoked, but because through the activity of thanksgiving, the goodness of God is publicly attested to and reaffirmed. By invoking such goodness, the world in all its complex wonders returns as a gift of God.

AN UNFINISHED ANATOMY?

I now turn to several questions raised for me as I worked with this material alongside Latisha's support-system friends; I have no answers for these questions, but they directly relate to how we understand the relation of theology to traumatic violence in today's world.

The first question concerns the *performative character* of psalmic interpretation. In his introduction to the commentary as well as throughout the body of his readings, Calvin repeatedly refers to his text as a "performance" and to himself as a "performer."[22] What insights might we gain into the nature and task of theological reflection if we took, as Calvin bids us, its performed dimensions more seriously? This question relates back to my initial claim that dramatic imagery captures, for Calvin, the true scope and function of theological discourse and its relation to scriptural exegesis. In this context, what does it mean to perform the psalms, to take their voice on as dramatic roles and to let them become the script of our action? Clearly, this raises important questions about the relation between aesthetics, theological discourse, and the nature of social action and practice. In caring for Latisha, could it be that she—and all of us together in my New Haven congregation—needed to collectively take on the task of performing with her, through art and music and drama, the three roles of psalmic performance?

Related to this is a second question. In this essay I have mainly focused on Calvin's written *Commentary on the Psalms*, but this commentary is not the only context in which Calvin engaged the poetic prayers of David. In the worship community of Geneva, Calvin regularly preached on the psalms in the afternoon service. Liturgically, they also constituted the substance of congregational hymn singing. In his Geneva articles on church organization and worship, Calvin describes this activity as a crucial part of the communal prayers that the faithful perform together with patterned regularity. As he explains it, singing the psalms edified them "so that the hearts of all be roused and incited to make like prayers and render like praises and thanks to God with one accord."[23] In other words, singing the psalms is one of the central ways in which Calvin imagined people *collectively* lifting up to God their innermost thoughts as well as their shared and spoken yearnings.

If my analysis of the Psalms and trauma were extended to include this dimension of psalmic practice, I would move more directly into a discussion of liturgy and the role it plays in the collective healing of traumatic violence. It may have been in the actual, embodied performance of the psalms that Calvin helped the whole body of Christ undergo a healing process that was as physical as it was emotional and spiritual. Might we imagine that by singing the psalms the church performed itself into a new and ever renewed form of embodied community? The possibilities for expanding our interpretation of the Psalms in this direction are exciting not only for our understanding of ecclesiology but for eschatology as well. Such a possibility bids us to consider the nature of hope performed and the physical, embodied dimensions of theological transformation. Although my own church was not able to take this step in dealing with the grief and trauma our parishioner suffered, in our own small ways even our ongoing individual interactions with her held a wisp of the promise of such engagements.

This brings me to a final question—a question less hopeful and more sobering to consider. Though it is inspiring to think of a group of people performing themselves into a new community through their collective reenactment of psalmic praise, we must face the possibility that these poems/songs might also be performed in a manner that forcefully reinscribes the violence articulated rather than healing it. From my earlier discussion of literature on trauma, we recall the claim that when persons experience overwhelming violence, there is often a tendency to compulsively reenact the original scene of the trauma without interrupting its dramatic unfolding. If this is true—if people who suffer traumatic events can become caught in a time warp where the violence done to them is constantly reenacted in the present, often in a manner unknown to them or in ways that pass as "normal"—it may well be that a community could use the often-vengeful rhetoric of the Psalms to fuel hate rather than transform it into healing praise of God. In my own congregation, this possibility was ever present in our temptation to respond to the harm our young friend had suffered by casting our children (and by implications, ourselves), more broadly, as the always-innocent victims of "evildoers" who haunt our neighborhoods. Although it was no doubt true that innocence and culpability could be unambiguously ascribed in her situation, the temptation to cast it as the score of a larger political drama is, I believe, not only misplaced but also socially dangerous.

PART 2

Crucified Imaginings

In this part of the book, I turn to the work of theological imagining—of writing scripts that might carve new paths through our imagination in the wake of shattering violence. I turn to old stories—to scriptural stories—as a resource for imagining a future that breaks the hold of traumatic violence on the mind and soul. More specifically, in each of the chapters that follow, I meditate on the story of the cross, and I consider its imaginative resources for the work of renarrating our world. Best read as three parts of a single story, these three interlocking reflections bring the central trauma of Christianity, the tortured death of God, to the center of the book—and ask how it is that "redemption" happens in its midst.

4

The Alluring Cross

> When all the crowds who had gathered there for this spectacle
> saw what had taken place, they returned home, beating their
> breasts. But all his acquaintances, including the women who
> had followed him from Galilee, stood at a distance, watching
> these things.
>
> —Luke 23:48–49

For anyone familiar with the Gospel passion narratives, the
basic shape of the crucifixion story is not hard to grasp; its contours come with almost instinctual clarity to those for whom it
matters. For those compelled by its truth, its claim is primal: it
pulls all of life and history into its consuming frame and fire.
Even though the time of its actual occurrence has long passed,
the mental gestures it grounds are as strong and alive as ever,
particularly in the interior worlds of those who believe it.

See it with me: There I am—there we are, all of humanity—
standing at a distance and gazing out upon at a horrific sight. A
man, gentle of spirit, fierce in heart, is nailed to a cross, tortured,
dying. There are people scattered around him, some good, others bad, others just present, beholding him as he in turn beholds
them. We see him, he sees us, and in the space between our
shared gazes, dark clouds are gathering. There is blood and urine
and gasping words and collapsing worlds, and then somehow,
suddenly, in the middle of it all, there is "redemption." The veil
parts and something new and good happens. Salvation comes.

If the story does not strike you as odd, then you have missed
a key element in its telling. The events transpiring are horrible.

When we see them in our mind's eye, we are not supposed to like them, to desire them, to find any sort of comfort in the pain suffered there. If we follow the proper plot line in the Gospels, the whole scene should repulse us, beg us to turn our heads away, stir within us disgust at its violence.

At the same time, however, we are told, oddly, that at the very moment the scene is most unbearably horrendous, it is also most redemptive. At its worst, it is its best. As we gaze up at this dying body, we are asked to find comfort in it, to desire its goodness, to embrace its hope. We are compelled, deep within, to believe that in the throes of this traumatic event, God uniquely meets humanity in the fullness of love and offers to us the grace of life abundant.

At the same time the violence repulses, it attracts.

There are other oddities as well. When this crucifixion scene unfolds in the space of our imagination, the mind's roving eye intuitively scans the whole stage in search of a figure with whom we can identify. We want a place to rest, a spot where we can settle in and say with familiar honesty, "There I am; that's me," a place to anchor our repulsion and our desire.

The story will not let us do this, however. The Gospel's narrative complexity keeps our internal world in flux, our identity shifting. One moment we are a weeping mother, a long-suffering friend, an abandoned lover: the next, we wear the skin of a shamed betrayer, a scavenging solider, a terrified devotee. Then, without missing a beat, we are up on the cross and looking down at our offenders, lifting up prayers, and wondering how it was that this horror came to pass. And then, in yet another leap of thought, we are up in the heavens, looking even farther down upon the scene, dissociated from its brutality, confident that all will be well. Where we land in the story changes as quickly as the thoughts and desires triggered in us by its characters and plot line.

We are here and then there. Sinners, saints, victims, God.

Over the centuries, theologians have returned to this scene again and again, trying to decipher the significance of these strange features: the simultaneity of devastating, traumatic violence, and redemptive promise, and the ever-shifting identities it scripts for us. No matter what they decide about its metaphysical significance, indeed, no matter how they analytically solve the riddle of the cross's relation to grace, the meaning that counts most on a day-to-day basis is the one nestled deep within the beholder's heart—and hearts are unwieldy and often unpredictable sites of meaning-making. The cross makes sense in ways that do not make sense. Imprinted on our conscious minds, it animates our unconscious compulsions and drives in ways that escape us. We live within the story but are not always sure quite how. We both know it and don't know it.

Herein lies perhaps the greatest peculiarity of all. We are obsessively committed to telling and retelling the story. We preach it, over and over again, in the hope that people will comprehend it anew and be moved. We write it over and over again in novels, poetry, and theater—we paint it, sculpt it, carve it, hone it, stitch it, sing it, play it—all the time hoping that if we repeat it often enough, we might succeed in unlocking its secret. In our personal lives, we go back to it time and again, sometimes seeking solace, sometimes righteous justification, sometimes just simple comprehension, yet each time hoping that in it we will find sense to our living. Clearly, it matters to us enormously that we understand. And yet, at the end of the day, we confess that the truth to which this horrific, fascinating event bears witness remains true even if we never hear it or believe it or find any meaning at all in its mysterious disclosure.

Grace is grace. It comes.

5

The Mirrored Cross

For the message about the cross is foolishness to those who are perishing, but to us who are being saved it is the power of God.

—the apostle Paul, in 1 Corinthians 1:18

The previous meditation on the alluring cross—the story of the cross in its confusing and yet compelling nature—is primarily abstract; in contrast, the story of the cross that follows is profoundly embodied; it begins with a story of women using their bodies to fight back against violence. I encountered this group of tough women several years ago when I helped to lead a women's self-defense class that met on Thursday nights in the all-purpose room in the parish house basement of my church. Although it was advertised in numerous church newsletters, I was the only properly church-active person in the class. Most of the others had come via referral from domestic violence centers around the city.

Not surprisingly, during the twelve weeks that we met, the dozen or so women gathered rarely spoke of things theological; mostly, we moved our bodies, learned to hit hard, scream loudly, and kick with force. And when we spoke, we either talked about the various forms of violence that had marked our lives (violence that some could not even remember) or proudly joked about the scraped knuckles we acquired from punching the walls of the room. All told, it was a wonderfully bonding and empowering event, and its force was lodged firmly in the physical world, where we fought together to empower our bodies against the wounds inflicted by the world.

The last meeting of the self-defense class, as it happened, coincided with Maundy Thursday. In the UCC tradition, we mark this day in a service that celebrates the Last Supper and tells, in gory Gospel detail, the long tale of Christ's betrayal, trial, and crucifixion—the passion play. As the service progresses, the lights in the sanctuary are dimmed until, at the end, only a single candle casts shadows on the cross that sits in the front of the room. It is quite a dramatic liturgy, one in which the theaterlike character of the crucifixion tale is made vividly apparent; ritually, everyone present is required to join in its reenactment, albeit metaphorically and prayerfully.

That evening, I was surprised when four women from the class appeared at the church's front door and slipped into back pews just in time for the start of the service. Two sat alone, two together, and as they lost themselves in the growing darkness of the liturgy, they all wept, silently, profusely. So did most others.

After the service, Mari spoke to me first, rubbing the knuckle she had bruised in class: "This cross story, . . . it's the only part of this Christian thing I like. I get it. And, it's like he gets me. He knows." She hugged me and walked out. Shanika left next, saying something about Jesus standing between her and her ex-partner, taking blows meant for her, keeping her safe. Sarah, her closest friend from the shelter, disagreed, smiling. "He's the King, man. He's throwing your ex's sorry ass in hell's jail soon as he can." Joanne, the last to leave, didn't say anything but gestured toward the cross with a slight shrug just before walking out the door.

Why did they come that evening? And what did they experience as they listened to the story and participated in the ritual? Why had this story—and *not* nicer healing tales or Easter's glad tidings—enticed them into pews? What was the appeal?

As a feminist theologian, my first reaction was to worry that somehow they had been inadvertently harmed by being there. I worried that as they sat there, they were once again being emotionally battered by bad theology; that by having to listen to the story, they were being lulled into believing that God was an abusive father who willingly sacrificed his son for the good of the world (substitutionary atonement); and that if they were beaten and sacrificed by abusive people in the future, they might believe they were undergoing something similarly salvific.

Yet I knew from our class that none of these women valorized or romanticized the violence done to them or to others. After all, they were learning to fight back against violence and in rather ardent ways, no less. Furthermore, they had as much as told me that the service was empowering to them, not devastating, and I had to believe that they meant what they said, that they could be trusted arbiters of their own sentiments. And it was not just their words but also their bodies that had spoken. Granted, each of them sobbed and shook during the reading. Each looked sad in the darkness that enveloped us. But when it came time to leave, they seemed neither diminished nor depleted: to the contrary, they seemed thankful to have been there, to have heard the story, and to have cried together.

Their reaction was not only *not* traumatic; it also seemed healthy, perhaps even healing. Rather than provoking fear, the story-ritual had nourished them. And as their departing words to me conveyed, that nourishment flowed from a strong, positive connection they felt with Jesus in the midst of his passion. Far from cultivating a passive victimlike reaction, their identification with him appeared to lift them up by bringing them down, and to strengthen their spirits by drawing forth tears.

What, then, did the passion play have to say to each of these women? Mari's comment struck me as significant: "I get it," she had said. "He gets me. He knows."

Although these words from Mari appear simple on the surface, they capture well a long and complex thread of Christian interpretations of the cross that highlight the believer's experience of solidarity between themselves and Christ as the source of redemption. *Imitatio*, recapitulation, the way of the cross, solidarity: for Mari, the passion play was a mirror of her own experience. Indeed, Mari's response indicates that there are key points of similarity between the trauma drama (the generalized story told by trauma theorists about the structure of traumatic events and their aftermath) and the passion play (the enacted tale of Jesus' march to the cross).

How does the passion play tell a tale that resembles the account of trauma outlined by theorists? First, both stories— the trauma drama and the passion play—originate in exactingly particular and insistently embodied events of violence that happen to individual subjects; and yet they also are both dramas that are publicly recounted in a manner that encourages others to find their stories therein. For both, the more deeply personal they are, the more universal and communally rich their power becomes.

Second, in both accounts the relationship between self and other is vexed in the extreme. On the one hand, both tell stories in which overwhelming violence is inflicted by an outside force that (usually a person who) violates all our usual boundaries of health and wholeness: the crucifiers in the one instance, the abuser in the other. On the other hand, both stories tell us that the only way to break the hold of this violence upon its victim is through the intervention of an external agent who, to some degree, also steps across the boundaries that normally distance us from others, to give us the help we need: God in one case, the therapeutic listener/witness in the other. In this regard, the external interruption of other people into our lives is revealed to be the necessary condition of both sin and grace.

Third, both grapple with the fragility of memory. In trauma theory, we learn that for survivors, the originating event of violence often goes unremembered; but in its absence, it remains constantly present to the self in the mind, in the form of nightmares and unnamed anxieties. In theologies of the cross, this dynamic of the presence of an absence is vividly described in theological accounts of Christ's descent into hell, when he goes beyond the border of history into the world of no time and disappears from our view.

Fourth, in both there is an acknowledgment that even though we do not "know" things in the usual manner when violence happens, we can still know the truth about it indirectly, albeit in neither a "the facts of the matter" manner nor a "just fiction" manner. In both, the true account of the violence suffered dwells beyond both the land of make-believe and brute data; it lives instead in a kind of third space—the space between the given and the imagined, between history and story, between event and dream. And because of this, both stories recognize that poetry rather than straightforward tale-telling is often the best way to capture meaning.[1]

Fifth, in both, it is crucial that the events of traumatic violence are testified to and then witnessed and believed by others in order for healing to take place. This healing involves, at least partially, the creation of a jointly authored story exposing the event of violence, which had been previously silenced, and then integrating this event into a broader life story. In both dramas, then, redemptive community emerges in the space of proclamation. In an event of speaking, hearing, and believing, a new future unfolds.

I list these five areas of insights into the shared character of these stories—the relation between particular and universal, the self-other relationship, the loss of memory, the failure of linguistic representation, and the dynamics of testifying and witnessing—because I initially believed they would provide me with the substance of the Christology I was looking for, a theology of the cross that would make redemptive sense of my self-defense friends' Maundy Thursday experiences. Yet the neat alignment between the two stories raises important questions about the limitations of this analogy. In many respects the trauma drama outlined above is simply too narrow to hold all the stories of persons and communities that it should be able to include. Or put slightly differently, when applied so broadly, the term "trauma" seems to obscure some of the most important differences marking the lives of the people it should be able to describe.

For instance, sometimes people remember traumatic events, sometimes they don't; Joanne recalled every detail of her boyfriend's beatings. For Shanika, her assault is a blank. Sometimes survivors are also perpetrators, sometimes they are not; Mari knew she had been a terrible mother to her two daughters; Joanne, however, was remarkably kind toward the children she cared for. And the differences proliferate. Sometimes a community may work to create public space for speaking about the events of traumatic violence, as in wartime situations or in the case of the World Trade Center; but sometimes a community may tend to prevent the public articulation of tales of trauma, as in the cases of incest and domestic violence suffered by most women in my group. At times, acts of resistance merely mimic the violence that created them—as in the case of Joanne's substance abuse; sometimes they do not, as in the case of Mari's bold prosecution of her offender. On occasion, an event of traumatic violence is initiated by the more powerful against those with less power—as in the case of Joanne, who was abused by her grandfather. At other times, the violence erupts from the margins toward the center, reversing, if only momentarily, the standard flow of power in a community, as was the case of a manager who was harmed when Joanne as a teenager was involved in a liquor store robbery.

The women in the self-defense class each had a different story to tell, even though the stories overlapped with one another; the more we talked, the better we became at telling these stories in ways that emphasized these overlaps. The difference between these stories was not just a reflection of difference between the trauma survivors' individual temperaments; it was also a reflection of different cultural contexts of meaning and of the different configurations of power within which the violence occurred and within which the present-day storyteller found herself.

As we listened to the women speak, it was similarly apparent that the way one tells one's story, the way one crafts the rhetoric of one's own trauma scene, can vary significantly depending on what one wants the story to accomplish, politically and socially, at any given moment. Sometimes we needed to give an account of what it meant to have been a *victim* of overwhelming violence and to come undone in the wake of its horror. Sometimes, however, we needed to tell the same story in a manner that cast us as *fighting feminists* who would "take someone down" if we needed to. Both stories could be told at the same time by a single person without any contradiction. It even seemed that the complexity of our lives demanded such double tellings.

If the trauma-drama narrative is unstable and multivoiced, it is also clear that theological interpretations of the cross are varied and mutable as well. As a theology professor, I know well the long list of models that Christian communities have used to explain how God saves the world through an event of traumatic violence: sometimes we say that Christ saves by being a blood sacrifice; at other times, we describe him as saving us by offering the world a moral model of self-giving love. Sometimes we insist that Christ saves us by exposing human sin in the act of being killed by humans; at other times, we preach about Christ as the scapegoat who unveils the lie of scapegoating. The list is long. As Savior, Christ is the one who does battle with the devil and, by tricking him, wins our release; Christ is the oppressed one who, on the cross, announces God's unrelenting decision for the poor; Christ is the one who in the moment of crucifixion shows us that even in the depths of traumatic violence, God stands in solidarity with us.

As a systematic theologian who is also a feminist, I am aware of the limits as well as the strengths of each of these accounts of the cross. When I consider the many ways theologians interpret the cross, I strongly reject any aspect of a theology of the cross that turns God into an intentional agent of traumatic violence; and I firmly believe that however one interprets it, the crucifixion both denounces evil and also announces the universal reality of divine love, of grace. But apart from these two constraints, my sense of which christological model speaks most powerfully to trauma shifts in relation to the stories of the survivors I read and listen to. Sometimes one story seems correct; at other times, a different interpretation more aptly makes the point that Christ saves.

This variability in the story of the cross was brought home to me poignantly one day when, in the course of a single afternoon, I listened to a World War II veteran and a domestic abuse survivor tell me dramatically different stories about their lives and about the cross. The vet described what it felt like to be a part of invading Allied forces that were "delivering and freeing" territories captured by Germans; for him the idea that God invades our world to deliver us from the captivity to sin made perfect imagistic sense. For him, invasion, deliverance, and grace were linked in the same imagined picture of God's loving action. The domestic abuse survivor, on the other hand, explained how she used to imagine that if Jesus were there when her partner hit her, he would have jumped in the way and taken the hit instead of her. She also imagined God holding her when she cried later, hidden away in her room. In her imaginings, Jesus was enacting a self-giving sacrifice that included the spilling of his blood for her, and he was also holding her in an act of divine solidarity with suffering. Here were sacrificing, holding, and grace—all able to exist in the space of the same cruciform image. Given her offender's violently invasive actions, images of a divine invasion were clearly not comforting to her; they held no aesthetic room for sin and grace to coexist. In these two stories, I saw two different trauma dramas interacting with at least four different Christologies, each of which made a kind of rudimentary sense to my own christological orientation.

When Mari told me that she saw her own story in the passion play, she directed my thoughts toward a Christology of mirroring: the mirrored cross reflects our story of suffering back to us. But that mirroring is clearly complex, more complex than a simple action of reflection. Given the multiple stories of the cross, how is it possible to offer a clear story to those who suffer? If there is no stable theology of the cross to offer to the trauma survivor, how can we preach it? Do we not need to give our listeners a clear plot line headed to a coherent ending in order to reassure them of God's grace, power, and love in the world? What resources might we turn to in order to make sense of so many shifting perspectives and so many particular, hurting lives?

To explore this, let us turn now to the Gospel of Mark's rather unusual and unended tale of redemption.

6

The Unending Cross

[The women] went out and fled from the tomb, for terror and amazement had seized them; and they said nothing to anyone, for they were afraid.

—Mark 16:8

For several years now, I have been asking how the church might more effectively minister to people who live through an event of overwhelming violence and continue to suffer from its emotional, cognitive effects. I have been particularly intrigued with the challenge of preaching about the cross to such people. Not only is there a question as to which story of the cross we might tell, but another important issue is also at stake: How can ministers craft sermons that speak to the plight of trauma survivors without retraumatizing them? How do we make theological sense of what happened on the cross in a way that speaks to the experience of traumatized victims without glorifying violence?

How might one put an end to the story of trauma by offering an answer to those seeking relief? In the final section of this three-part reflection on the cross, I turn to Mark's Gospel to respond to these questions. Ironically, Mark's Gospel is a story of the cross that ends without a proper ending. Recall that Mark concludes his story of Jesus' crucifixion not with a grand resurrection scene but with a group of horrified women running away from the tomb, pledging to say nothing about it to anyone. Mark leaves the story of the crucifixion hanging in a kind of suspended animation; we readers are left wondering what happens next, and we receive no clear answers.

Mark's Gospel thus disappoints our expectation of receiving an ending to the story. But perhaps it is worth reflecting here on the very concept of an ending. For most of us, when we hear the word "ending," we imagine something like the last chapter of a murder mystery in which we learn who perpetrated the crime and in which all the heretofore mysterious clues and inexplicable events are revealed to be part of a single logical narrative. The "end" is the final installment in a chronological narrative. While this is a useful way of thinking about "ending" (and one I will sometimes use in my own reflections), there is another way to understand what an "end" is. In classical Greek philosophy, *the "end" (telos) of something is described as being the ideal form that a given entity is designed to take.* The "end" of a piece of wood designed to be a table is the form of tableness.

This notion of "end" can also be applied to the human life. As a person of faith, I believe that the form or end of our lives is to flourish as the creatures that God created us to be, and for our lives to bear witness to the grace that God has bestowed upon us. Our end is the form of God's glory. For Christians, this end is not just something we strive to reach in the last chapter of our lives. Rather, it is a possibility that breaks in upon us every day: it is the shape of faithful living; it is the form of a beautiful life. Accordingly, to ask about the relation of endings to trauma is not only to ask how we might write the last chapter to a story of violence but also to ask how we might tell stories about violence that in their very *form or genre*—throughout their narration—bear witness to God's forming grace and mercy. This means that endings are as much about aesthetic substance as they are about chronological conclusions. They are as much about the graced possibilities of imagination that preaching can open up for people in every minute of their lives—they are as much about this as they are about writing satisfying and conclusive endings to stories concerning the completion of our lives.

Turning to Mark's Gospel, then, allows us to consider the relation between these two senses or meanings of the term "ending": the end as a lived Christian life, and the end as narrative conclusion. Of all the events narrated to us in the Gospels, the original ending of Mark's story is perhaps one of the most pastorally confusing. Recall the well-known scene. It begins with three women coming to the tomb to anoint Jesus' body, a task that is not very surprising; at the time it is what women did as a matter of course for those they loved. They prepared them in death. But in this scene, Mark lets us know right away that the situation is not as self-explanatory as it initially appears to be.

First, Mark indirectly lets us know that they are quite pious women; he tells us that they waited to anoint Jesus until the Sabbath had passed. Imagine waiting to care for the body of one so beloved until the "proper" time arrived: it must have required incredible strength of faith, and a good deal of managed frustration and grief, to sit and wait until the right moment came.

Second, we are told that the women are up and wandering around the countryside in the early morning, likely leaving home before sunrise, moving through the gloom of early dawn. Maybe they are trying to keep their journey a secret; maybe they are afraid of being seen; we are not sure. Whatever the case may be, with this detail, Mark casts an ominous air over the scene. There is little light to see by, no map to follow.

Third, he tells us that the women are talking about who will roll the stone away. We find out that it is a very large stone, a fact that makes their journey seem quite irrational. From the start they were ready to undertake a task they knew might be thwarted. With this small detail, Mark makes the women appear weak in muscle and mind. They may not have thought things through, but this detail adds an element of suspense. Will these pious, ill-prepared women, creeping about a cemetery at dawn, accomplish their mission?

As a good storyteller, Mark immediately resolves some of the tension for us while at the same time creating more. They arrive and discover, to their amazement, that the stone has already been moved: a small miracle. But then another possibility must be crossing their minds: thieves or their beloved's enemies could be lurking and could seek to harm them as well. Such a threat is real. At the very moment that Mark throws the women into the world of these inexplicable events, he casts upon the story shadows wherein violence haunts the possibility of miracles.

The women do not linger long in this indeterminate space, however; they immediately enter the tomb. Is this a bold move or the foolish act of hysterical women caught in the grip of the unknowable? Whatever their reason, the next events are so startling that this question no longer matters. Sitting before them is a young man. He is sitting on the *right side*, and he is wearing *a white robe*. These are strange details for Mark to give us: it is as if Mark wants us to really grasp this odd occurrence, to ensure that we vividly hold this unbelievable part of the story in our imaginations, this moment in which we discover that the body of Jesus is gone and an unexpected herald has appeared in its place. At the instant we encounter a mysterious absence, we confront an equally unexpected presence.

The startling man in white then speaks. Mark lets us hear his speech, but it is not what one might expect. He delivers his message in a rather straightforward, matter-of-fact manner. He does not speak in the elegant prose one might expect from an angel given a role as important as this. The young man simply tells them that Jesus is not there because he has risen; they are to leave, tell the good news to the other disciples, and then go to Galilee, where Jesus will be waiting. It is as if he is reporting the nightly news: the Nazarene is "going ahead of you," he says, "just as he told you." Into the midst of the bizarre and unbelievable thus come words that feel unusually solid, earthen, commonsensical, and self-evident, even though the events they narrate reflect a reality that reaches far beyond the ordinary. As readers, we can begin to feel the ending drawing near, and as Mark pulls us into the young man's words, we are allowed to believe that what happens next will be not only surprising but also satisfying. If Mark continues in this vein, our ending could well be as delightful as it is amazing and as down to earth as it is heavenly. The tension in the narrative could not rise any higher nor expectations of resolution become any stronger.

What we next discover, however, is far from satisfying or amazing. Mark does not offer any of the things we are waiting for. Rather, he gives us a brief and disappointing description of the women's pitiful response. They turn, in fear and astonishment, and flee. They run out of the tomb. They scatter *in silence*. Complete silence! Why? Mark answers this question for us directly, hiding nothing. They are *afraid*, he tells us. The Greek makes it clear that this is not the kind of theological "afraidness" that we think of as "awestruck" or "full of wonder." It is the kind of "afraidness" we usually think of as "scared"—the terror that comes after a violent, overwhelming event, a traumatic fear. They are frightened speechless. And in their terror, they fall mute and run. As they do, the Gospel message itself seems to dart away from the tomb, off down the road, and out into the space of oblivion.

And then Mark stops the story. At the very moment when we, as readers of the Gospel, are in need of the greatest relief; at the moment in which we are supposed to witness the event of proclamation that launches Christianity into its future and hear about how the first people of faith really experienced the resurrection—Mark does not give it to us. Instead, he depicts a group of weak, irrational women who fall silent and run away. In doing so he allows the Gospel story to run away from us. Instead of pulling it together, he leaves us peering into the gaping space of an ending that never comes.

Mark's nonending is unnerving. Indeed, it is so unnerving that in the early days of the story's circulation, other Gospel-tellers decided to add a nicer, more appropriate ending to the tale. We find that ending in the canon we now read. It begins right after this "unending" and is written in a voice that is completely different from Mark's, but it gives you everything one might want in an ending. Jesus does all the things expected of a risen Lord; he appears to his followers, plans out their future, and allows them to see him ascending in glory to heaven. It is not hard to imagine the relief that a first-century Gospel

audience must have felt when someone finally got it right.
Jesus rises, we see his risen body, we hear his resurrected voice
telling us what to do, we watch him go up to heaven, we see
him sitting next to God, and feeling empowered, we go forth
and do as directed.

It is easy to understand why other writers added this ending.
Then and now, *we like our stories to have satisfying conclusions.*
In the midst of life's many uncertainties, tragedies, horrors, and
chaos, we want the Gospel stories—like all important stories—
to provide a narrative that brings a sense of transcendent order,
direction, and meaning to our daily actions and to our understanding of God. We want stories that allow us to get on with
things, as if there is an ultimate point to it all, a conclusion to
the tale of human life that makes it worthy of living. *As any sea-
soned pastor knows, the task of preaching consists of precisely this:
of inviting people into the stories, which, if proclaimed with passion and wisdom, provide them with just such ordering frames of
reference.* This task is even more essential in the case of pastoral
care for people suffering from trauma. Helping people of faith
find a tale of compassion and grace in the stories of God's good
news, a story capable of giving manageable shape to their many
griefs and angers—this is central to the pastor's more intimate
role as counselor and guide to the broken and the searching.

Given our penchant for good endings, what then are we
as pastors, theologians, pastoral care providers, and people of
faith to make of Mark's original ending, the ending that never
really comes? How are we to preach it? How are we to make
it pastorally alive? In recent years, biblical scholars and theologians have offered a variety of answers to this question, suggesting different pastoral solutions for the minister who grapples
with this uncomfortable text. The most common interpretation is that the women's faith was eventually strong enough to
override their fears: they ended up telling people that Jesus had
risen. How else would the church have gotten started? Therefore, as people of faith, we are allowed to be startled, afraid,
and grief stricken to the point of silence, but if we persist, our
voice will eventually return, and we will be able to find our

faith again. The practical message embedded in this interpretation is a message of Christian *perseverance*.

Another common interpretation of Mark's abrupt ending argues that Mark wanted to leave the ending open so that we, the readers, would feel that we are responsible for making sure the Word is lived and proclaimed anew in our own voices, as our own story. As such, this interpretation offers a pastoral message of *hope* and *empowerment*. The empty space at the end is not the space of fear but the space of welcome. The Gospel message is ours to hear, ours to proclaim, and most important, ours to live, each generation in its own way.

A third common interpretive answer to the problem of the ending holds that for Mark, the cross, not the resurrection, is the theological center of Jesus' story. The meaning of the story was displayed on Golgotha, where salvation was made possible. The resurrection confirmed that it *was* God who died on the cross, and it should be proof enough that an angel appeared to proclaim this; we do not need to directly see the risen Lord, as we needed to witness his crucifixion. From a pastoral perspective, the message here is that fear can become awe when we realize that Jesus died for us. Whatever befalls us, we are called to express *gratitude* and *humble prayer* for all that has been done through Christ's atoning death.

All these are powerful examples of how to make theological meaning out of a seemingly inconclusive narrative ending. When viewed from the perspective of pastoral theology, there is much to commend in these readings. But should we only preach interpretations that smooth out the roughness of the women's silence and fear? Will the text support these readings, or does it ask for something more difficult? Might there be times in the life of ministry when the truest meaning of Mark's Gospel is discovered not by smoothing it over but by actually engaging its absent ending, its ruptured narrative, its lack of final order? Could it be that this "unending" is part of what this text has to teach us?

In order to see what Mark's lesson in unendings might be able to teach us about proclaiming the gospel to the traumatized imagination, consider the preacher's distinctive role in shaping imagination. In classically Protestant terms, preaching is most centrally an activity aimed at expanding and deepening the congregation's imagination of grace such that we might be better equipped to live in and move through a world understood as a place of God's continued, unfolding grace. Here, grace is understood as the unmerited love of a God who desires that we flourish and who gives us the power to seek such goodness. In this regard, preaching is an embodied, incarnational activity, a lively example of the "Word-made-flesh" in order that the glory of God's grace might be vitally experienced and known.

Understood in these terms, preaching assumes particular importance in relation to the traumatized individual for whom the narrative of grace has disappeared or withdrawn from the world of their lived experience. Violence has a traumatizing affect on one's capacity to imagine grace, particularly in relation to language. Trauma can fracture our speech, and speech without the right tone or attitude, language without gesture, hampers our capacity to think expansively about life in general because it puts us in spaces marked by fear and constructed for protection. As such, fractured speech can profoundly hamper our capacity to imagine a reality that runs counter to the logic of traumatizing violence, the logic of a grace that opens, that secures, that invites one to wholeness.

There are two specific features of this fracturing that I want to highlight here because of their pertinence to preaching. First, traumatic violence often leaves holes in the stories we tell about our lives. There are places in those stories where endings are abrupt and ragged, other places where stories are unfinished; in this way, violence creates open-ended narrative spaces filled with fear, silence, and uncertainty. As we have seen in earlier chapters, one of the principal features of a traumatized memory is that it keeps reliving the trauma and often cannot find an ending to the story. When this happens, one can get stuck in time, a place that trauma theorists refer to as an "eternal present," a place with no past and, even more tragically, no future, no direction toward which life unfolds. In this regard, violence cuts off thought midstream and leaves one stranded in midstory.

The second feature of the traumatized imagination relevant to understanding the role of preaching is the loss of a person's sense of agency and, along with it, a sense that one can positively affect the world through the intentional acts of speaking, gesturing, and moving. For people who have found themselves helpless in the face of overwhelming violence, there often continues to be—long after the events of violence have passed—a feeling that one does not have the power to make decisions and carry out desired plans. At the very moment one's sense of time gets frozen midstream, so too one's sense of meaningful action comes unraveled.

Viewed in the light of these two features, the task of preaching takes on new dimensions. We like endings to our stories, particularly when those stories are of Gospel proportion. What is the task of preaching if not to tell the Gospel story in a manner that makes its ending particularly vivid and powerful? Moreover, the power of the story's ending gives order to its beginning and its middle. Jesus' life and death make sense to us—they have an understandable order to them—because in his resurrection we find an ending that pulls it all together. In this view of preaching, however, how does one take into account the "unending reality" of traumatic experience? How do you preach comforting endings to people who live in the pain of an eternal present? How do you preach resurrection to an imagination traumatized by the terrible finality of violent death?

Similarly, the task of preaching, at its best, is often aimed at empowering people to make better constructive decisions about their lives, decisions that more accurately reflect God's will for the flourishing of creation, decisions that flow from a recognition of the abundance of grace in their lives and the lives of others. What does it mean to preach with an expectation of influencing decisions and actions in a context where the capacity to speak and act has been disabled? How does one proclaim the call to follow Christ to people who cannot even imagine following their own most simple desires?

Mark's uncomfortable ending—his unending—gives us a clue to this mystery in the very silence it provokes. In this story we find a script that calls, not for oratory and powerful rhetoric, but for silence. In that space of silence there is room for a deeper kind of speech: the language of gesture, of embodied communication, of the pouring out of soul in flesh that transcends the power of language to capture or define it. In Mark's unending we have a script for *performance* that gives us new insight into the grace of preaching to the traumatized imagination.

"When we say 'performance,'" writes David Rhoads, "we mean the whole event of a performance in the ancient world. The text, the experience of the performer, the context or situation, the social location of the performer and audience, and the experience of the audience"—all these are taken into account.[1] Part of our difficulty with Mark's text is due to the fact that we have not paid adequate attention to the rhetorical and performance conventions that surround the formation of Gospel traditions. The intended ending of Mark's Gospel may not be the Greek preposition *gar* (for). Mark may very well have intended that the ending be a *gesture*. The ending of Mark's Gospel takes us to the very limits of language, where we cross the threshold into silence. Why? To show us, by means of a gesture, an embodied image of fear. To see what fear looks like, one need only look into the faces of those who have been traumatized by violence for an image more haunting and eloquent than words can convey.

The ancient performer,[2] looking at the abrupt ending of Mark's text, may have understood Mark to mean, "Gesture here." "Gesture" meant a wide range of things: a stance, a posture, or a facial expression to convey thought and attitude. "Ellipses" like those in Mark's ending were commonplace in the literature of Mark's day and signaled to the text's performer that interpretive gestures were called for.

To turn to the clues and hints by which a reader can detect the author's intended performer reading aloud and gesticulating, what are they? They are absences or gaps. What the words seem to say is incomplete or contrary, syntax is irregular, and at the same time, there is no evidence that words are missing because of physical damage or copyist's error. In such cases, a reader can often make better sense by adding in thought the import of a nod or a wave of the hand.[3]

So what do we imagine might be a gesture appropriate to this text? And how does this insight inform our interpretation and our preaching? Whatever the ancient performers did with this text is of course irretrievable. But one can certainly interpret the text through the performance conventions available to us. To do so, the interpreter takes on the persona of the narrator by speaking the words of the text and by suggesting through embodied, expressive speech the actions, attitudes, and points of view represented there. In this way the interpreter and the audience experiences the text in the same way that people first experienced it—as performed utterance.

A student gave a performed interpretation of this text in class as part of her preparation to preach from it. She worked closely with the Greek text to develop her performance, and for the last verse, she used a literal translation of the Greek: "They said nothing to anyone. They were afraid, for." When she filled the silence after the preposition with a *gesture,* the rendering had evocative meaning. She had shrugged her shoulders as she reached with her arms out to her audience, almost as if she were pleading with them. Through her performance the class *experienced* the story as unfinished and incomplete. In that place, her face, her stance, her gestures were images of fear, puzzlement, *terror,* reflecting the reaction of the traumatized women in the story, but also displaying in bold relief the human anguish of the question that became the spine of her sermon: *What does all this mean?*[4]

The discussion that followed her performance was rich and compelling and offered fresh insights on this text. The familiar text became unsettling again as students wrestled with some basic questions: *Why were the women afraid? What is it about the news of a "resurrection from the dead" that is terrifying?* We know how to live in a world where death has the final word; it is the only "absolute" we can be sure of. We know how to order our lives and go about our business. What happens when life has the final word? To admit to what this text claims—that there is "resurrection"—is *traumatic!* "What if death is not a reliable absolute?" asks Tom Troeger in a sermon on this passage. "Then thè comfort of knowing that life is a fixed and closed system is called into question. If death is overcome, if the one indestructible certitude that marks existence is shattered, then reality is wide open!"[5]

For victims of violence, life has become a "fixed and closed system" that the *language* of the gospel of Jesus Christ may not be able to penetrate. Mark's ending teaches us a lesson: when sacred rhetoric meets the embedded realities of traumatic images, perhaps silence, accompanied by *gesture*, is the only appropriate response. What *gestures* might be called for to "finish" the sermon on this text? What gesticulations can we use from our ritual and liturgical traditions to enact our expression of fear, anxiety, or hope?

Preaching the ending of Mark's Gospel brings us to the limits of language and leaves us on the threshold of silence. Scripture does not fear the descent of silence after language fails. Judeo-Christian faith teaches that it was within a silent void that the Creator began the drama of creation, fall, and redemption, not unlike the silence at the end of Mark's Gospel. Who is to say that anxiety was not within the Creator as the volatile uncertainties of time and space were set in motion? Faith teaches that creation began with a spoken word, and yet "word" cannot be extracted from "gesture" or "performance." As Dominic Crossan puts it: "In the beginning was the performance; not the word alone, not the deed alone, but both, each indelibly marked with the other forever."[6] What God performs in the silence before creation is the subject of the gospel. It is a gesture toward redemption and restoration that renders the Creator vulnerable to the contingencies and chaos of the unfolding human story.

<hr />

In a darkening church lit by one faint, flickering candle, women sit weeping in the deepening shadows of the cross.

Silence speaks to silence as the story gives way to gesture; the scattered, terrified women at the tomb are present with us in the sobs of other women who have known terror, who have felt the shattering power of violence. This liturgical gesture connects the women, and it also transforms their stories. One story opens the space for the other; because of the silence in the unending of Mark's story, there is room for the embodied experience of the women from the self-defense class. In this space there is no need for a well-formulated Christology packaged in a singular ending. Sitting in the darkening space of the candlelit church, perhaps the women from the self-defense class experienced the power of gesture and performance to speak to the silences in their own stories. The shadow cast by the cross becomes a dark womb that holds their brokenness and envelopes their pain. In this space there is no divine justification for suffering, but there is the outstretched gesture of understanding, of solidarity, and of welcoming embrace. When Joanne turned to me, to tell me what the passion play meant to her, she shrugged—without words, but with an embodied understanding of the story of trauma.

Learning from Mark's Gospel, preaching the Gospel, especially the passion, to those traumatized by violence becomes an act of performing an imagined space where the power of embodied emotion is acknowledged. Such preaching moves, as the women did, toward the tomb—with fear and uncertainty—and acknowledges what Mark does, that God's gospel cannot ever be finished. Its edge is unsettling and unnerving. It brings us to the voids and chasms in our experience where gestures of grace are imagined and at long last embodied. In these voids and silences we find we are not alone: we are in a vast landscape of grace, broad and beautiful enough to hold all the fracturing of our lives, and in so holding us, to give us back ourselves made whole.

PART 3

Ruptured Redeemings

In each of the three chapters that follow, I explore what the work of recovery and healing entails in relation to the theories of trauma and the ruptured theological imagining that I have discussed above. In particular, I am interested in examining the workings of grace in the lives of individuals who have suffered from trauma and finding the ways in which trauma survivors can allow grace to speak to and within their own lived experiences.

7

Sin, Creativity, and the Christian Life

Rachel and Mary in Traumatic Embrace

A voice is heard in Ramah,
  lamentation and bitter weeping.
Rachel weeping for her children;
  she refuses to be comforted for her children,
  because they are no more.
                                        —Jeremiah 31:15

Here am I, the servant of the Lord;
let it be with me according to your word.
                                        —Mary, in Luke 1:38

In the history of the Christian tradition, two major themes structuring Christian faith-imaginations are *creativity* and *sin*. In this chapter I consider the way in which trauma impedes one's capacity for creativity and thus opens a complex terrain of sin to the victim of violence.[1] More specifically, I suggest that viewing trauma as an experience of brokenness and of banishment from the resources of language, imagination, and creativity enables us to understand sin as neither exclusively social nor individual, but as simultaneously collective and individual—as both structural and personal. In what follows, then, I discuss sin in ways that are both traditional and new, ways that draw upon theological tradition, and ways that offer new passages through that tradition, most particularly for those who have felt themselves irretrievably touched by the experience of sin as traumatic harm.

SIN

I begin with a number of propositions: First, discussion of sin should serve to strengthen Christian faith, not weaken it. In

how this creativity might best be enacted. When we live faithfully, we seek to mirror God's own creative intentions for the
world. This is *faithful creativity*, creativity in its truest form. If
our creativity manifests forms of life that thwart God's divine
will for human flourishing, however, it is sinful. When this
occurs, our creative actions are corrupted and distorted, and
true creativity fails to be expressed and enacted. Yet by living
in conformity with God's intentions, we act in ways that please
God, delight our Creator, and hence delight and enrich the
whole of creation, including ourselves. We then embody or
image what the tradition has referred to as "the glory of God."

What exactly does it mean to "embody the glory of God"?
In a well-known phrase, Calvin refers to creation as "the theater of God's glory." In making this reference, he suggests that
when we look at the beauty and complexity of the vast world
around us, we should be awed by the breadth and depth of
God's own beauty displayed within it. Glory is thus something
that both God and the world share. God creates it, and we see
it, participate in it, and hence "bear it." The phrase conjures
up images of the world shimmering and shining with marks of
God's grace, a world handcrafted by a wondrous divine artisan,
a world that shows forth the marvel of God's own blessed goodness. This glory not only describes the manifest brilliance of
creation; it describes even more perfectly the beauty displayed
in Jesus Christ, the revealed embodiment of divine glory in its
greatest splendor. In him, glory marks our understanding of
both creation and redemption.

Glory is something apprehended not just intellectually but
also through the full range of human senses; it is imaged and
embodied. You can taste, touch, see, feel, smell, and hear it. As
such, glory has as much to do with form, shape, and substance as
it does with ideas. When something in the created world bears a
resemblance, at the level of material form, to God's own blessed
intentions for the world, it is physically "glorious." The term
thus highlights the distinctly aesthetic dimensions of God's creative work. When the world shimmers and shines with God's
glory, we experience it as aesthetically pleasing or beautiful.

When we embody God's glory (God's creative intentions) in our acts of creativity, we too participate in making our lives and our world more beautiful places, places that radiate with graced possibility. Hence, it is fair to say that when we are faithfully creative, our acts are beautiful reflections of God's glory—be they the work of cleaning the house, grading papers, or hiking through the park. Even more vivid are those explicit forms of artistic production—painting, writing, weaving, dancing, and so forth—that we undertake as expressions of our ongoing engagement in God's intention for creation. In other words, when we are creative—faithfully creative—the glory of God is made concretely present in the beauty we see and feel.

Graced creativity is important, and comprehending its obverse is equally crucial. When we exercise creativity without imagining God's creative intentions, we risk constructing a hyperreality that has no relationship to God's desire for the restoration of the world. When divorced from imagining what God desires, creativity produces fantasy worlds that serve as escapes from reality. Creativity grounded in imagining the glory of God leads us to participate, as people of faith, in creating a world that we believe is possible (despite appearances to the contrary).

Because history has proved that creativity has been used to construct fantasy worlds rather than to imagine a world that embodies God's glory, people of faith have sometimes understood creativity as antithetical to the good. To be good, to be religious, to be faithful—such is precisely *not* to be creative, in this understanding. Here one might understand oneself to be responsible for signing on to God's agenda, but certainly not in any way to imagine what this might entail or to think of oneself as integral to it, embodying God's glory.

Unfortunately, this separation of the good from the beautiful, of faithfulness from creativity, has led to the misconception that the good is boring. According to the Roman Catholic theologian Hans Urs von Balthasar, for example, "'the good' has lost its attraction because it is cut off from beauty."[2] By contrast to this, however, an incarnational faith insists on pursuing the beautiful, or "imagining embodying the glory of God" by realizing our identity as creative agents. Again, as von Balthasar puts it: "Though beauty and being have become separated in the modern imagination, their integration was accomplished in Christ, the true Word and image of God, who was not only believed, but seen."[3] When thus conceived, creativity as imagining embodying the glory of God leads to the transformation of sinful structures that rob us of life. As Belden Lane puts it, citing J. R. R. Tolkien, "In a world [that is the product of the imagination], one encounters the unexpected breaking in of joy beyond the walls of a world bound by fear and despair."[4] Creativity propelled by imagining embodying the glory of God leads us to embrace the work that brings God's kingdom to earth as it is in heaven.

Understood in this way, creativity raises a number of interesting questions about the nature of the Christian life and its goal of embodying God's glory. How do we, as human beings, act creatively in ways that are both faithful and beautiful? Moreover, how does our creativity unfold in ways that are not only in principle good for the world and ourselves but are also concretely pleasurable to us, ways that delight us and bring us joy? And in related terms, how do we respond to situations where our creativity is misdirected or distorted, situations either where we create in ways destructive of human flourishing or where we are so harmed by others that we cannot create at all? How does sin affect our creativity, and how might we create in the midst of sin, our own as well as others?

I am particularly interested in the question of how sin affects the creativity of women given Christianity's association of sin with human embodiment, sexuality, and oftentimes, femininity. To explore the question of the relation between sin and creativity, particularly as it pertains to the lives of women, here I propose five theological features of the self are crucial to our creativity: (1) *agency*: our God-given capacity to act and hence to be creative; (2) *time*: our God-created capacity to imagine the future and to remember the past and—within the space of these—to compose our lives; (3) *voice*: our created ability to

articulate and embrace our particularity, our call to be individuals with unique gifts to offer in the context of community;
(4) *permission*: God's divine gift of forgiveness that allows us
not to be perfect but to live nonetheless in grace as we creatively act and express our particularity; and (5) *call*: the gift
of Christian vocation, the reality that we are each called to live
in faithful relation to God and others in this graceful dance of
creation and creativity.

OUR SCRIPTURAL COMPANIONS

How might we think theologically about the relation between
sin and creativity, particularly for women? Following the insight
of John Calvin, who described Scripture as the "lens of faith,"
I have imagined the story of two women—a story designed to
serve as a "lens" for thinking theologically about trauma, sin,
and creativity. The tales of their lives are quite different from
each other and yet juxtaposed with each other; emerging from
each are insights that illuminate starkly different but interrelated features of both sin and creativity as they are played out
in Christian existence today.

❧❧❧❧❧

Imagine, if you will, the unexpected meeting of two women
on a dusty road on a hill, outside the walls of Jerusalem. They
are the same age and, in their youth, could well have been mis-
taken for sisters. Their encounter is brief. They are not even
aware of each other as they draw near: each is too lost in her
own world of grief and memory to take in the presence of a
stranger.

The taller of the two women is not crying; she is standing on the side of the road, wrapped in a tattered red cloth,
staring off toward the hill's horizon where three bodies hang
nailed to roughly constructed crosses. Her face bears a blankness that bespeaks feelings too enormous to name. Her frame
is etched, still, unmoving, frozen against the hot afternoon sky.

The smaller woman is walking away from the hill, her body swaddled in mourning black, her back turned to the crosses. A friend walks close by, holding her up, helping her take steps; she stumbles frequently, her face streaked with muddied tears, her eyes closed.

At the point on the road where their paths cross, the woman in black stops to rest. Suddenly overcome by waves of grief, she begins to cry into the shoulder of her accompanying friend. "My son." The other, red-wrapped woman, momentarily startled out of her numbed reverie, looks in the wailing woman's direction and immediately knows who she is. All of Jerusalem knows her. Without moving, the startled one begins to mouth the same words, as if speaking a mantra worn thin through years of repetition, "My son, my son." Their eyes meet for a brief moment, and we wait to see if they will speak.

Who are these two women? If we had met them in their younger years, they would have been alive with creative energy, young mothers exhausted but hopeful about the future stretching before them. But such is not the case today.

The smaller of the two is Mary, the mother of Jesus. In Scripture, she is depicted in her youth as a meek but powerful peasant woman who is called to bear Divinity within her, the quintessential model of creativity. Vitally alive and vibrant with possibility, she visits Elizabeth and gives voice to the Magnificat, a song of hope in which she boldly embraces her strange calling to embody God's glory (Luke 1:46–55). Walking down the road from Golgotha, however, she now looks different, her demeanor far from bold or exuberant. Propped up on the arm of her companion, broken by grief, she stumbles away.

The other woman, let me call her Rachel, is never mentioned in Scriptures, but a woman's life much like hers most surely has existed, perhaps in numbers too large to imagine. Her own lifelong crucifixion began long before Jesus even set his eyes toward Jerusalem. She is the victim of a genocidal war crime that happened to her in her youth, a survivor of the Slaughter of the Innocents, the horrifying event that, as the Gospel tells us, followed upon the birth of Jesus. As she watches the man called

Jesus crucified on the cross, it is hard to know by her expression whether she is relieved or grieved by his execution. She has a scar running across her face, left by a soldier's sword on the day they came to her village and in a brutal act of state-ordered terror executed her two-year-old son, her only child, her beloved offspring. Standing on the road, she sees Mary weeping and feels envy that this woman at least saw her child grow to maturity. If she realizes that this is the one for whom her son died, perhaps she feels his execution is justified.

Sin, creativity, and the Christian life—how do we think about these things together? One answer lies in thinking about Rachel's and Mary's stories both separately and together, the stories of two women whose parallel lives brought them, that afternoon, to the cross of Jesus—and to each other; two creative souls whose youthful voices give us both the verdant poetry of Luke's Magnificat and the tragic lament of Jeremiah's wailing woman; two women whose pasts tell us much about their future.

Rachel's Story: Trauma and Creativity

Let me begin with Rachel. How does this woman's imagined story frame our thinking about creativity and sin? What can our construal of her experience allow us to see about the place of brokenness and grace in our own lives?

In contemporary theology, there are two major images for sin. As indicated earlier, we often define sin as morally bad acts committed by individuals; if we are broad-minded, we couple this with an understanding of social sin as the reality of larger structures of oppression that diminish the flourishing of humanity. But Rachel gives us a third picture of sin, one that stands in the gap between individual agential sin and structural social evil. She allows us to see, in painful detail, what a particular form of social sin called "traumatic violence" does to individuals when it inhabits their reality. Rachel gives a picture of the self unraveled by the sinful destructiveness of our world, the self upon whom terror has fallen, someone to whom sin has happened and within whom the consequences of this sin are embodied in profoundly intimate ways. In other words, she gives us a view of sin that is simultaneously collective and individual, both political and private. Moreover, she gives us a view of sin that allows us to see the complex ways it affects her capacity to be creative and to embody the glory of God.

In efforts to understand this dimension of our human experience of sin, the insights of trauma theory are enormously helpful. As we have seen, traumatic events never happen in exactly the same way, and the people who experience them never feel their effects with identical force: however, the literature on trauma tells us that there are remarkably similar features that seem to cut across the large spectrum of violence that produces trauma. If we interpret the damage that traumatic violence does to people as a form of sin that "befalls" them and that they are then compelled to "live," then how might we construe the connection between this form of sin and the Christian call to be creative? To answer this question, I return to Rachel's story.

Imagine Rachel standing on the hilltop, wrapped in an old, worn, ruddy-colored silk cloth. The cloth covers her from head to toe, shielding her from the world around her. It seems to be holding her together, albeit in a ragged, tattered fashion. Thirty-one years ago, Rachel wove this cloth on a loom in her home near Bethlehem. In her youth, she was widely known as one of the finest weavers in the area, celebrated for the intricate designs of her fabrics. But since that day, a day she cannot remember, her hands have been unable to touch the loom. The loom gathers dust in the corner of her room, the child's tunic she was making rotting between its braces.

Today, she twists this remnant of her former brilliance in her hands, wringing its ragged edges tightly. The cloth that holds her is wearing thin. She has begun to think she is too old to create again, having lost the most beautiful creation of her life, her child, to a calculated act of state-sanctioned violence, a military sword, in the land we now call the Middle East. She is the fractured creative spirit of many: wounded, unable to bear forth the glory of God that is in her.

What Has Befallen Rachel?

First, let's look at her sense of *agency* in light of what we know about the long-term aftereffects of traumatic violence. The clinical literature tells us that trauma often leads to feelings of utter powerlessness, feelings that reflect the powerlessness experienced in the original event. Imagine Rachel on that fated afternoon: when the soldiers came to take her son from her arms, she tried to hold on to him but could not. She tried to stop them but could not. She struggled against them but failed. In the days that followed, Rachel slowly lost the capacity to imagine herself as an actor in the world at all. She lost the sense that she could intend an action—one as simple as feeding her child—and then complete it, see its effects, and take responsibility for its consequences. But she now lives in the prison of a victim's imagination. Not only are intentions and actions severed in her mind; action itself has also become a burdened possibility, one enjoyed by others but not by those who, like her, are dead of soul.

Second, what of Rachel's sense of *time*, her capacity to envision a future and remember a past and, out of this, craft a present? The literature on trauma tells us that the events of violence often lead to memory loss. Not remembering is, actually, to remember an event that was too overwhelming to comprehend even at the time of its occurrence. In Rachel's case, there are only fragmented memories of that day. When she hears a barking dog, she often flashes back to a horrified blankness. When she smells fish cooking, as if it were that morning, she feels nauseous. When she hears a child cry, her mind freezes, her hands shake. Having lost the past and her will, the future becomes not a place of expectation, but just further space into which she is forced to move, to tread out her years in depressed isolation. To be able to weave, to create beauty on her loom, she not only needs to imagine that her actions matter; she also needs to imagine that her creative work has a future. She cannot.

Third, to be creative, a person needs to have at least a minimal sense of personal *voice*. This can take the form of knowing that one has a substantial body or a bounded identity. It involves knowing that you are "somebody" with something to say, something to create. In contrast to this, trauma survivors often dissociate; they psychically disconnect their minds from their experiences of embodiment. They become numb and often lose a sense of the boundaries that mark the edge of self; they become unable to distinguish where they end and others begin. In Rachel's case, this unboundedness is symbolized by her inability to weave new clothes to cover her body. She cannot craft a shawl capable of enveloping her, warming her, protecting her from rain and cold and the pitying stares of others. She has only a worn rag to adorn her, a rag left over from the days when her hell began. She has been, it seems, strewn into the world.

Fourth, when Rachel was learning to weave, she grew to see that imperfection was inevitable and that she had *permission*, as an artist, *to fail* or to not "get it right" as she worked her craft. Sometimes a thread would snap as the shuttle passed across the taut strands of her warp, sometimes the silk would tear or a wool thread bundle into knots; and because the color of the dye was never even, she learned to find beauty in its shifting hues and not an imagined evenness. Accepting these flaws was key not only to Rachel's ability to find pleasure in the movement of her loom but also, and even more important, to have the courage to keep working when the material she created did not exactly realize her design. But thirty years ago, this all changed. When we see her standing on Golgotha, we see a Rachel who has replaced that forgiving discipline of heart and mind with another, unforgiving habit of thought that keeps her hands frozen, her heart cold. As with many trauma survivors, she finds herself constantly replaying the events of that day in her imagination—the fractured parts she remembers—and trying to get the ending right, trying to fantasize her way to a different future in which her son lives. The compulsion to repeat haunts her sleeping as well as her waking. In her anxious search for a perfect ending to a story she cannot undo, she remains perpetually caught in its mimetic replay of horror. For her, imperfection has terrifying consequences; its costs are so high that she cannot embrace even its possibility. And in her refusal of that possibility lies her prison.

Finally, if Rachel were alive today, what of her calling and of the Christian notion of *vocation*? What of the theological claim that faithful creativity will have as its telos the glorifying of God and the flourishing of community? What of Rachel's capacity for understanding her life as having a direction and her ability to see that direction intentionally unfolding in the context of community? To answer this, recall that she is standing completely alone on the roadside; Mary is the one with a companion. Recall that survivors have a hard time forming relationships with others because their fundamental trust in the world has been violated. Could it be that when Rachel looks over at Mary and the followers of Jesus who surround her, she is puzzled by what she knows of their devotion to him and the deep friendships among them? In contrast, she cannot trust anyone enough to form friendships or join a group, much less concentrate long enough to have listened to and understood one of Jesus' sermons or to have committed herself to a movement. As for her faith, yes, she is by tradition as Jewish as Mary. But what does that mean? She was born and will die in a land marked by imperial domination, and it is because of her Hebrew ancestry that her son was slaughtered. Had she been Roman, he might have lived. Or even more painfully, had she been Mary, Yahweh's angels might have helped her escape. Who could believe in the God who did not come to her but saved others instead?

And so here we have Rachel, a woman cut deeply by the ravages of sin. Tighter and tighter she wrings the cloth between her hands as she stands on the roadside, her eyes moving between the hilltop's dead and the fallen, weeping woman near her. She twists the cloth she once created, unable to even imagine a new creation. A new life? A new shawl that she might wrap around her for comfort and warmth? For beauty? She is unable to fathom the mere possibility of what it is she no longer has. Caught in sin, she cannot see sin. Broken by violence, she does not know the depths of the evil that still inhabits her body and soul.

Mary's Story: Blessing and Creativity

The story of Rachel illustrates how the sin of inflicted, traumatic violence undoes us as creative personal beings who embody the glory of God. The story of Mary offers the reminder and the hope that sin need not always have the last word. As with Rachel, Mary's relationship to sin is complex. Though we know more about Mary than we know about Rachel, there is a great deal about Mary that we are forced to surmise. Since she was born into poverty, she is traditionally imagined as little more than a slave—a young girl who (being female) spends her hours and her days on menial tasks. Like Rachel, then, she is affected by the systemic sin that marginalizes her due to her gender and class. And even though she has not suffered the trauma that Rachel has suffered, she has, no doubt, been socialized not to think highly of herself: She averts her eyes, leaves the speaking to others, and endeavors to serve the men around her. Certainly she would never think of herself as a prophetess, the bearer of the One who would save.

And yet somehow she comes to understand herself differently. Mary—a peasant girl—is called "blessed" by God. Even more incredibly, she eventually recognizes and lives into the reality of her blessedness, contributing to the very work of God. Mary's story gives hope that while social sin has a detrimental impact on the embodied existence of creative agents, it need not, finally, determine who we are, how we understand ourselves, or what we do with our lives. Mary demonstrates that recognizing one's identity as a sinner can simultaneously precipitate actions that are both creative and transformative.

Informing this reflection on Mary are feminist studies on the subject of "feminine sin" (a term first coined by Valerie Saiving).[5] Historically and sociologically speaking, "feminine sin" is what women are most apt to be guilty of when marginalized by sinful power structures. Given the message that they are second-rate citizens who do not have the capacity to shape or influence culture as agents, women too often accede to the message conveyed to them by way of these sinful systems, internalizing these false assumptions as their own. Women, then, are often not assertive enough precisely because they have become the passive creatures they were taught to be. They do not act forcefully enough because they have accepted that they are incapable and weak. They are frequently too hard on themselves, do not think highly enough of themselves, or are unable to perceive themselves in relation to the events that surround them.

How is it that women can move from being trapped not only by the sinful structures themselves but also by their own internalization of these sinful structures? How can "living into their identity as sinners"—recognizing the role they play in these systems—actually *propel* creativity on the part of women? To address these questions, I return to the story of Mary.

Imagine Mary, venturing forth to scrub the laundry in a nearby stream, when she is visited by an angel, who tells her that she is "favored" and that the Lord is with her. Mary is immediately "perplexed,"[6] and for good reason. What could an angel want with her, a poor girl with nothing to offer? And so she "pondered what sort of greeting this might be."[7] With women who, through the ages, have not recognized their value, Mary is looking over her shoulder to see who else Gabriel must be talking to. But the message, and the fact that it is being addressed to her, becomes only more difficult to fathom. Mary will bear a son, and he will be named Jesus. "Of his kingdom there will be no end," Gabriel declares to Mary.

"How can this be," Mary naturally asks, "since I am a virgin?" Gabriel does not argue with her. He does not try to convince her of her capabilities and potentials. Instead, he reminds her that "nothing will be impossible with God."

"Let it be with me according to your word," Mary responds. "Here am I, the servant of the Lord."

Scripture encourages us to imagine that Mary emerges from that encounter a changed woman. She is pregnant with new life, and she begins making traveling plans. She envisions a new world in which sinful power structures have been overturned. And she who was voiceless lifts high her eyes, fills her lungs tight with air, and opens her mouth to proclaim this great, redeeming reversal.

What Has Gotten into Mary?

First, let's look at her sense of *agency*. What is it that moves Mary from a posture of self-effacement to the position of an agent, creatively participating in and proclaiming the coming of God's reign? At first glance, it might seem that the visit of the angel precipitates the change. It is easy to assume that anyone who has an emissary of God pay them a visit and assign them an important mission might immediately imagine themselves as powerful beyond measure. And yet Gabriel's first words to Mary do not provoke this sense; rather, they reveal her profound sense of inadequacy. "How can this be?" she asks. "Not me," she states, as if she considers herself incapable of the task at hand.

It is not initially clear whether Mary's declaration of her incapacity is a manifestation of feminine sin or an exercise of self-awareness. Is Mary buying into the systemic presumption that a young woman has nothing to contribute? Or is she accurately assessing her abilities and resources in the face of the news set before her? Perhaps both are at play. There is a sense in which, ironically, Mary's position as a marginalized figure in the social system makes her more open to acknowledging that what she is called to do far exceeds her, or for that matter, anyone's regular productive capacities.

What if it is precisely Mary's recognition of her incapacity to create, in and of herself, that positions her to do the impossible? Read this way, Mary's response reminds us, at this point, of the Reformed doctrine of "total depravity"—a doctrine that has too often been used to impede agency rather than to foster it. The story of Mary illustrates what happens when we understand this doctrine not as disparaging human beings but as recognizing the condition they find themselves in. As Paul Lehmann puts it, the doctrine of total depravity "simply expresses the fact that whatever it takes to overcome the ethical predicament of humanity does not lie within the powers of humanity." Rather, Lehmann insists, "Human renewal . . . comes to humanity as a gift."[8]

Mary seems to understand this. Whatever it takes to bear the child she is called to bear does not lie within her power. She knows her virginity, her depravity. And this recognition—this recognition of her sinful condition—prepares her for receipt of the gift of renewal.

One mark of Mary's renewal as an agent is her changing sense of *time*. Understanding her depravity, Mary is reminded by Gabriel that, though engaging in this creative work of bearing Jesus is impossible, God has made what is impossible to be possible. Things are not as they seem, for God is at work in history, subverting and reversing that which is right before our eyes. As Mary will soon articulate, the impossible things God does are done for us and with us, creatively replacing those paradigms that we have presumed are the only possibilities. "God . . . has filled the hungry with good things," Mary will proclaim. "[God] sent the rich away empty." Knowing her depravity, being reminded of the power of God, Mary is suddenly not stuck indefinitely in the present, without reason to believe that there is anything beyond the tasks she does today and the ones she will repeat tomorrow. Mary can now see a future, a future that lays claim to her in the present, a future that includes her as an agent of transformation. Mary's belief in a transcendent God, far from entrenching her in her own sense of depravity and incapacitation, frees her to remember the past, envision the future, and act in the present.

As a creative agent in relation to the incarnational event, Mary claims permission to be someone she has not been socialized to be, someone who is not a victim in relationship to the systems that claim her; rather, she contributes integrally to the shaping of a new world. The permission that she takes hold of lies at the interface of her recognition that she is incapable of this creative task, in and of herself, and her recognition that she can do the impossible, for God has made it possible. Luther famously told Christian believers that they should "sin boldly" and "love God more boldly still." Mary—a sinner in love—claims permission for behavior that is otherwise impermissible.[9] To give birth, as a virgin? To go on a journey to unfamiliar places? To speak, prophetically? Freed from the pressure to be perfect, Mary steps forward and engages in these audacious, creative acts. She does what she cannot do and is simultaneously called to do.

As an emerging agent who sees the future moving into the present, Mary claims permission to have a *voice* in a culture that understands her as (and no doubt trained her to be) voiceless.[10] Yet the sins of sexism and classism do not, ultimately, keep Mary from being "somebody with something to say." Importantly, Mary's discovery of voice does not entail a sheer overpowering of everything that stands in her way. Rather, Mary's voice emerges in the context of what feminist theologians call *naming,* or what traditional Christian theology calls *confession.* In short, Mary identifies the situation for what it is, in all its complexity. She teaches us the power of confessing not only our personal sin but also sin perpetrated against us.[11] She herself is sinful, she has been victimized by sin, and still God has blessed her. Mary finds her voice as she faces up to and celebrates who she is in relation to the events and circumstances of her life. Because she owns up to who she is, she is able not only to imagine a different future, but also to envision her place in it. "All generations will call me blessed," she insists, recognizing the role she is playing in the present moment and as a creative agent.

Mary's story demonstrates, finally, how to live into our *vocation* as beings created and re-created by our Creator God and endowed with creative abilities ourselves. She knows that her contribution to the divine enterprise is not contingent on how much energy she can muster, despite the obstacles she faces due to personal and social sin. Rather, Mary's creative engagement in the incarnational event is founded in God's claim on her as an integral participant in the divine artistry.[12] She is, to speak in the terms of Dorothee Sölle, an "irreplaceable" agent whose work is valued not because it has been assessed and deemed worthy of inclusion, but because Mary herself is claimed and included for who she is.[13] As one who is blessed and lives in recognition of her blessedness, Mary embodies the glory of the God whom she also bears to the world. Imagining the shape of God's kingdom, she steps forward and speaks poetic, prophetic words that are absolutely—also—hers.

MEETING GRACE, GRACED MEETINGS

Rachel and Mary present dramatically different stories of trauma and creativity. For Rachel, a woman undone by sins that befell her, the possibility of being a creative, active, life-embracing person seems to be a promise beyond her reach. For Mary, a woman with intimate certainty that she is blessed, the possibility of embodying the glory of God seems already an accomplished fact, although it is sharply challenged by the grief she experiences in relation to the suffering of her son. The first (Rachel) gives us sobering pause; the second (Mary) gives us honest optimism. The first speaks to the places in everyone where harm has banished hope; the second speaks to the sites where sparks of creativity continue to ignite and inspire even in the midst of pain and loss. Two quite different worlds of imagination, two very different spirits of possibility.

In closing this chapter, let us return to that roadside on Golgotha and explore what happens when the women met: What words passed between them when their radically different experiences of grief were brought face-to-face with one another? If speech did not come, what might their glances have expressed about their hopes and fears as they stood in the shadow of the cross? What might the sheer presence of the one have offered to the other, wanted or not?

Rachel to Mary

What does Mary learn from Rachel? What can a person who has been so blessed possibly learn from one who has never glimpsed a reality in which sin does not have the final word? Mary has spent thirty years pondering, with wonder, her inclusion in the work of God; Rachel barely has the resources to recognize her violation. Perhaps Mary resists identifying with this broken woman she meets on Golgotha. Perhaps on some level she is petrified that the fraction of joy she has managed to salvage will be rendered obsolete by the dull gaze of this woman. Surely the two cannot have much in common. One's son has died a boy; the other is dying a man, and this makes a difference. Mary has known, with her son, the joining of souls as well as the sharing of her breast. Together they have pondered the story of his birth and the mystery of his powers. True, the distance between them has grown during three years of ministry. But on the rare occasions when their eyes meet, she still knows that she has done the work of God in bearing him, raising him, and directing him to be—like her—a source of life to others.

In her better moments, Mary still believes that somehow, in some way, God will use her son to save her people from their sins. Embracing Rachel as a fellow sufferer would surely jeopardize all this. To acknowledge the penetrating impact of sin, especially in relationship to this one who came to save, would be to cast unbearable doubt on the promise of salvation. To know the insidious connection between the death of Rachel's son and the life of her own—that Rachel's son was killed in a search for Mary's son, who was spared, at least for a few years—would surely join the two women (or drive them apart) in ways too intimate to be risked. Better to stay silent, to nod politely, to continue traveling the long, endless road alone. Better to keep one's hopes intact, however small.

But perhaps Mary is still strong enough to risk learning from Rachel, to be reminded, again, that not all the hungry have yet been filled with good things, to be reminded that the greedy powers are all too present—killing myriads of children, indiscriminately, for the sake of their own security. Rachel's story teaches Mary that the reversal to which the Magnificat bears witness is not the reality of everyday existence in a fallen, sinful world. Though Mary's prophecy that sin is not enduring may be true, so is Rachel's observation, made by way of her persistent presence, that sin endures.

The hope to which Mary clings is actually far more endangered by Mary's resistance to what Rachel has to teach her than by her embrace of it. If Mary does not learn from Rachel, her creative engagement as an agent who can imagine a different future runs the risk of being mere fantasy. If Mary does not listen to Rachel, her bold proclamation that sin is not the end of the story becomes mere denial rather than relevant hope. Her creative words would, then, be antithetical to the good, for their goal would be to escape reality rather than to recognize what is beautiful in real-life creaturely existence. Rachel reminds Mary that the power of embodying the glory of God lies not in simply transcending circumstances or surviving grief. As Mary has periodically known in her life, but as Rachel teaches her again: God's glory is known incarnationally, in the depths of our bodies, at the point of connection with the most unlikely of all.

In embracing Rachel, Mary learns that one cannot have great hope without simultaneously bearing great grief. Mary must, then, learn again from Rachel about the brokenness of the created order that can, from the perspective of the Magnificat, only be named and mourned. From the context of this imagined world, a prophetic word of condemnation is uttered: *two-year-old children should never be killed.* This brokenness— this sin that surrounds us and lures us into complacency—will never do. Only as we confess it does healing become a possibility. Creative imaginings then become vehicles of this healing rather than perpetuators of pain.

In our grief as well as in our hope, we embody the glory of God, for our grief bears witness to what *should not be* and therefore to what *actually is* and *should be*, according to God's creative and redemptive intentions. This is what Rachel teaches Mary, in their imagined encounter. And Mary is then able to claim her own grief as a symbol of hope, a defiance of sin, an impetus for acting creatively toward the imagined future that has laid claim to her. With the help of Rachel, Mary moves away from the cross with no neutrality in relation to her circumstances. She is a mother who has watched her son suffer and die. And this should not be.

Mary to Rachel

What does Rachel learn from Mary? What gift of insight might the mother of Jesus have given to this broken soul? Alas, the answer to this question is difficult to fathom, given that the most realistic response is more tragic than inspiring. It may be that although Mary has gifts of wisdom abounding, Rachel cannot receive them. The harsh truth of our world is that many of the traumas we suffer are never healed or even identified. Perhaps Rachel never returns to her loom, perhaps the events of that afternoon on Golgotha will disappear from her mind like so many other memories, . . . and her shawl will simply wear thin and finally shred into nothing. It is a likely scenario.

But perhaps it is different. Maybe something new happens there. Maybe, standing there, Rachel is able to catch a glimpse of grace, a fleeting hint of redemption, a sense of the hope that long ago faded. If this is what happens, what might it look like to her, this grace that saves, this knowledge of sin that reconciles and opens up creativity, this love that might allow God's glory to shine in her? What kind of grace is capable of meeting her loss?

The Reformed tradition often refers to two features of God's grace. First, grace is a free gift; we cannot earn or even imagine its reality before it descends upon us in the fullness of mercy. Described as *prevenient grace*, it breaks upon us from the outside, disrupting our expected habits of thought and our most accepted forms of heart. Second, grace never violates us but rather cooperates with our capacities, enlarging our imaginations and expanding the borders of our usual actions. Described as *enhancing grace*, it is a power that moves deep within our being, sharing our plight, conforming to our reality, and in that identification, opening up new avenues of experience and hope. In both ways, grace bears the double mark of being at once a new, freely bestowed, externally composed gift and a deeply familiar, intimately known presence—a grace both foreign and indigenous to us.

When Rachel looks up the hill to the cross that afternoon, imagine this *enhancing, prevenient* grace being communicated to her as she looks toward Jesus dying on the cross. Perhaps she is able to see in Jesus a form similar to hers. Cruciformed, he embodies the fractured, tortured shape of her traumatic existence. When she sees herself in him, there is an identification of being that makes communication possible. There is a familiarity of form that allows him to be as close to her as she is to herself. He wears not only her ragged cloth but also her confused mind and lost memory. Her invisibility is invisible in him. Invisible, that is, until he gives public expression to her private wounds. "Who is my mother?" he mouths. "My son, my son," she echoes into the blankness of her past. In bearing her story, he brings voice to the horror she herself cannot speak. He is, in other words, her embodied testimony.

There is more to this exchange of glances, however, than testimonial identification. Not only does she see herself in him, she sees him seeing her. She is seen by him. He witnesses her; he receives her unraveled testimony-of-a-life as an offering of truth, and in that exchange, he articulates her unspoken history, her invisibility made visible in his eyes. In this play of visions, the reality of enhancing grace opens before us. He assumes her reality, speaks the unspeakable in his own loss of speech, and then returns all of this to her as he witnesses to what she believed would be forever unknown. Perhaps, in that moment, she remembers. Perhaps she does not but instead is able, for the first time, to accept the blank of history as her truth.

And still there is more, a plentitude of exchanges in this unfolding meeting of grace. Not only is there perfect unity of form between them, but also in the space of their shared trauma, he offers her something new: an advent, of sorts. Here prevenient grace breaks upon her, offering her more than a comforting solidarity and a conformation of knowing, enhancing presence. In some unfathomable motion of form, he shows forth glory in the very moment—his dying—at which the loss of divine beauty seems most complete. He bears the image and presence of grace—he somehow shines—in ways that Rachel, in her ragged cloth, seems incapable of consciously embodying in herself.

Wherein lies his glory? Is it in his awareness of God's presence to him in the midst of his suffering? Does his glory lie in his knowledge of its reality? Perhaps, but for Rachel this seems to be insufficient, for it is precisely her own capacity to know that has been so profoundly ruptured by sin. If his salvation of her rests in his knowledge, then he would only save her in the space of his knowing-difference from her. Where would the solidarity and identity be here? If this is not the source of his glory, could it then be in the singular unity of his will with the Divine, his obedience unto death? There is also a problem here—for Rachel, at least. Her own agential identity has come undone. If he saves through his will, then again, he redeems her only in that moment wherein his assertion of agential humanity is distinguished from and not identified with her. If this is the case, then the mirroring ceases, and it appears that to bear the glory of God, he must leave behind her traumatic world. Where, then, do we find that dimension of grace that conforms without violating? That embraces without threatening? If not in knowledge or in action, where do we find Jesus' glory?

Perhaps it is somehow in the form itself, its beauty, the material embodiment of God in his crucifixion; perhaps this is, to her, the shape of salvation. Not just any beauty: it is the beauty of love, the form of beatitude, that she sees in him. The traumatic violence he undergoes does not annihilate the form of his loving, although he bears within himself the full weight of the terror she knows. This love has no corollary, no mimetic twin. It simply is the truth of that moment, in all of its inexhaustible particularity. And the good news it reveals to her is that even if she never knows or acts as the creative, glorifying woman she was created to be, her glory shines nonetheless. It shines in the inexhaustible and brilliant particularity of her existence, in all its horrifying, lost details. That glory is simply the truth of her life. What could be more unexpected, more unmerited, than the sturdy reality that in God, she is loved; she is glorified by God and glorifies in God in the fullness of her loss. Her hands need not weave rich cloth, her future need not depend on past memories she will never reclaim; her acceptance by God— God's trust in her—transcends and thus renders impotent her nonexistent trust in others.

It may seem an unsatisfactory answer to the challenge of her traumatic sin, the sin that haunts her every breath. It may not be existentially sufficient for her to live in the space of a grace that loves without manifesting itself as transformed agency or as robust, confident knowledge. Maybe not. But one can imagine that it might be so.

Imagine, if you will, that in the moment when Jesus' form bears such glory, and she glories in his glory, between her fingers she pulls on the threads of her former craft and feels again the slight pleasure of creating something. As she pulls the strand more tightly, she moves toward Mary, the Magnificat now humming in the whisper of air that blows through her ragged shawl, not through Mary's youthful heart. The poetic genre of Mary's words becomes in its shape the genre that best annunciates Rachel's emerging voice —a broken form holding a hallowed truth, the aesthetics of grace. This fractured speech from Ramah is now what the grieving mother of Golgotha awaits to hear. In this strange communication, there in the heat of the afternoon sun, glory shines.

8

Hope Deferred

Theological Reflections on Reproductive Loss

It had been raining all morning, and the earth gave way softly as Wendy and I dug into it with spoons from her kitchen. We were quite a sight: two women, huddled under a black umbrella in the corner of a yard, digging . . . and crying. Wendy had been bleeding for three days, and she looked ghostly; she had just miscarried an eight-week pregnancy (her fourth) and was grieving not only this present pain but also her dimming hope of ever having children. In her grandmother's handkerchief she had collected a few small remnants of her loss—a combination of bloody tissue and dashed dreams. We placed these in the earth and tried to think of something profound to say, but words would not come. Having spent years together in a women's group at our local church, we were accustomed to praying to God in the feminine. But today, lifting up prayers to "Mother God" seemed a cruel joke, and we felt bereft as we struggled to find other theological images that might hold us in this moment. We were and continue to be strong advocates for "women's right to choose," and so praying for "a lost life" also struck us as wrong; and yet as feminists, we desperately wanted images that might bind us with our sisters in this time of loss and grief. But nothing came. Caught in a rift, our words fell unspoken into the grave we had carved out of the dirt, and I remember how very alone we felt.

We were far less alone than we imagined, however. According to the American Society for Reproductive Medicine, 6.1 million Americans presently experience infertility (which represents 10 percent of the childbearing population). Additionally, 25 percent of women of childbearing age will experience a miscarriage (not including abortion), and one in eighty pregnancies will end in a stillbirth. As these statistics suggest, many in our society share the experience of Wendy. It is endemic and widespread. And yet it remains a topic that North American public discourse continues to address only in cold clinical terms, if at all.

This is particularly true in two communities of discourse that cross the lives of Wendy and myself, the feminist community and the mainline Protestant church, two places where one might expect to find powerful resources for reflecting on the character of such loss in the lives of women (and men). The absence of such reflections in these places is, therefore, especially striking. In this essay, I address this particular silence by bringing the experience of reproductive loss into conversation with two fields of thought in which I work: feminist trauma theory and systematic theology.[1] My hope is that by bringing the insights of these discourses to bear on this experience, we might begin to better understand not only why such painful silences surround reproductive loss but also what resources are available to help us think about this issue, both as individuals who suffer this loss and as a broader church that seeks to understand it.

How might theory and theology help? That morning in the rain, Wendy and I did not first and foremost yearn for a conceptual argument about such things as divine providence or feminist notions of freedom (although each topic, in our later reflections, became enormously important). What we yearned for was more basic. We wanted images, a drama, a story, a vivid language that could draw together our strange experience in the rain and the faith and feminism, which have so profoundly formed us. What we sought, I believe, was the barest outlines of theological, visual poetry.[2] We needed a form or a genre of knowing that, crossing the multiple borders of our complex lives, could give meaningful shape to this particular event. As women of faith, we understood our lives as unfolding in the presence of divine grace; but caught in the force of this event, we were hard-pressed to "see" how reproductive loss found its place in this unfolding. As such, we sought an image that might allow us to "see" this vividly; a compact visual, a drama that we could imagistically inhabit as we asked: What does Wendy's body look like in the space of this unfolding grace? How might she imagine the future here? And who is the God who holds her body and her hope in the folds of this grace?

In the following pages, I will take the reader on a rather circuitous journey as I try to answer these questions and offer a rough outline of such poetry. In the first part, I outline difficulties in defining "reproductive loss." In the second part, I lay out the principal features of the experience of such loss as women who have gone through it have narrated them to me. In the third part, I describe "three tales of the self" frequently used by feminist theorists, and I explain why each dramatically fails to include the reality of reproductive loss. In the final section, I turn to the world of systematic theological reflection and begin to mine its resources for challenging this failure. As such, this chapter engages in the work of bringing theological imagining to bear on the lived experience of trauma—and reproductive loss is a trauma shared by an extraordinary number of women in our world today. Reproductive loss raises enormously important philosophical questions about the nature of the self, and it does so in a manner that allows feminist political theory, trauma studies, and systematic theology to engage one another in interesting ways. My work as a theologian stands in the space of that engagement: reproductive loss is a topic that enables serious reflection on the traumas embedded in the everyday lives of those around us and the theology one might bring into play to imagine grace breaking into the space of devastating loss.

DEFINING "REPRODUCTIVE LOSS"

As with any exercise in theory or theology, one's first task is to define the topic upon which one is reflecting, to circumscribe its boundaries. With the subject of "reproductive loss," I have found that this task is more difficult than it might first appear.

In the grief literature on reproductive loss, the three topics usually treated are infertility, stillbirth, and miscarriage.[3] In clinical terms, infertility describes a biological condition in which conception cannot take place (although it is often expanded to include biological conditions in which a fertilized egg cannot be sustained in utero for any number of reasons, including genetic ones); a miscarriage (often referred to as spontaneous abortion) is the loss of a pregnancy after conception but before twenty-four weeks; stillbirth is the loss of a pregnancy any time from twenty-four weeks to term in which the fetus dies in utero or immediately following delivery (in many such cases, the fetus must be "delivered" either by Cesarean or vaginal birth, and hence the term "still*birth*").

While these definitions provide helpful biological descriptions of the three topics I treat here, they do not address what I consider to be the most important dimension of the experiences for my purposes: the subjective experience of the women for whom these biological events become the occasion of grief. More specifically, I am interested in looking at the experience of women who desire to have biological children, who are biologically unable to do so, and who experience this bodily inability as failure, a desire thwarted, a loss of a potential child they hoped for and expected. In other words, I am focusing principally on women who (1) want to have biological children and try to do so, (2) are physically unable to do so, and (3) feel this inability to be a profound loss. According to the grief literature, the mourning that ensues when these features are present, as in the case of the three forms of loss I mention above, is distinct.

Describing the focus of my reflections in this manner makes it clear that I am concerned here primarily with this experience as it affects women and, hence, not men. This selective focus is not meant to imply, however, that men do not grieve such loss; many do, and they often grieve in ways quite similar to women.[4] There are, however, differences in men's and women's embodied relation to this kind of loss and hence differences in their texture of grief; my selective focus on women allows me to highlight the features of their grief particular to their embodied reality. My description also makes it clear that because I am interested in women who try to but cannot biologically reproduce, I am not going to deal with reproductive loss associated with abortion. Though it is clear that many women go through a period of grief after an abortion, their grief does not usually include mourning the failure of their body to either conceive or carry a pregnancy (although it does often include a profound sense of being betrayed by one's body).[5] Some women who choose to terminate pregnancy do not think of it as a loss, and in such cases, the event does not necessarily occasion grief.[6]

Having said this about the experiences I am not including, I must also add that those experiences included in my definition are more complex than one might first think. Their complexity appears on several levels. First, wading into the murky waters of "subjective experience" is an exercise in ambiguity. I have said that I look at women who "want" to have biological children, yet what it means to "want" something is quite complex.[7] Anyone who has realistically contemplated the prospect of having a child knows the reality of competing and often conflicting desires about its possibility: One can both want and not want children simultaneously. Not surprisingly, women who experience infertility, stillbirth, and miscarriage often feel similarly conflicted about the loss. Further, I am looking at women who in their grief experience the death of a hope, the thwarting of an expectation. But like desires, human hopes are always multiple, conflicted, and persistently indeterminate. Our motivating expectations and hopes are not always as clear to us as we would like them to be. At times we are not even aware of their presence, even in cases where they quite dramatically shape the character of our daily living. This is particularly true with respect to hoping for the birth of a biological child.

Related to this, the experience of grief associated with infertility, stillbirth, and miscarriage never occurs in a vacuum. It
is always socially mediated. It is a grief, which like all griefs is
shaped by its cultural context, and this cultural shaping occurs
at many levels.[8] For example, recent feminist work on the
topic of motherhood helps us appreciate the degree to which
women's sense of failure around not being able to bear children
is related to powerful cultural assumptions about the value of
motherhood.[9] To grow up a "woman" in this culture is to grow
up formed by a thickly gendered identity script wherein one's
body is assessed in terms of its treasured capacity to give life
and thereby to make one "a mother." To be a full woman is
thus to bear children and then to lovingly raise them. Admit-
tedly, this script takes different forms (often theological ones)
depending on one's social location, and it thus affects a person's
self-understanding in different ways and to varying degrees.
But even in the context of these differences, the force of this
construction is strong, its pull virtually inescapable. Because
of the advances of feminism, many women now have social
permission to resist this pull; but even in such cases, its power
remains, if only at the level of unconscious expectations that
are continually reinforced by dominant social and theological
images of women as mothers.

Tied to this is the fact that the women whose experience I
am exploring live in a culture that measures a person's value
according to what they "produce" or "make," be it through
the labor of body or of mind. Formed in an economic system
that thrives on a rhetoric of "efficient production," our culture
identifies persons according to what they do—what commodity they produce, be it a theological education, a car, or a Web
home page. Related to this is the view that as agents who creatively make things, persons are capable of and responsible for
making the terms of their future (this understanding of persons
has deep theological roots).[10] Persons have thus come to expect
that they should achieve the particular future of their desiring,
albeit one imagined within limits (but limits that do not usually include the reality of reproductive loss). In such a culture,

to experience one's body as "unproductive" is consequently to experience the body as a social failure and to view the hopes that were tied to this body as a failure as well.

I lift up these two constructions, motherhood and production, because they frequently emerge in women's description of their experience of reproductive grief. However, there are numerous other constructions that craft women's hopes and body images and hence the contours of their experiences of grief in these situations. For example, feminist theorists have done extensive work in recent years uncovering the often-racist features of these two reproductive myths: they expose the many ways in which our culture valorizes Euro-American motherhood while demonizing the mothering bodies of African American women and Latinas.[11] Similar dynamics follow the lines of class and ethnicity as well, showing ever more clearly that political stakes transverse our images of maternity and nurturing womanhood.

There are also other factors that affect this experience of grief. The advent of new reproductive technologies has dramatically raised women's expectations for successful pregnancies and deliveries.[12] Home pregnancy tests now make it possible to name a "pregnancy" within days of conception, thereby increasing women's actual experiences of reproductive loss—moving it far ahead of the culturally sanctioned "quickening," which marked the beginning of pregnancy until only recently. Further, the age of women having their "first pregnancy" has also risen in recent years, thus increasing instances of infertility and miscarriage. Feminists working on environmental issues have also made us aware of the threat that ecological degradation brings to women's fertility.

I offer this list of social and cultural factors that play into women's experience of reproductive loss because I believe understanding them helps women (and men) better respond to the complexities of this experience. By naming these factors, however, I have complicated the task of this project. I have strong theological and feminist reasons for questioning many of the scripts that mediate, for women, the experience of reproductive loss—particularly those social myths that lead women to feel that if they cannot produce children, they are not only failed women but also failed persons. In light of the harm caused by such views of women, it is crucially important that work like mine not exacerbate their power by unquestioningly accepting them, and I try not to do that here. I also believe that we need to have a much more politicized understanding of how reproductive technologies are used and how we respond to the racial and environmental dimensions of infertility.[13] As such, I do not want to bury these issues in my more subjectively focused analysis of the experience of reproductive loss. This is difficult to do, however, because this project tries to honor women's stories of loss, no matter how uncritical, irrational, or "unfeminist" they may sound. This involves listening in a manner that resists the urge to simply reduce the experience of grief to an account of its social construction. Granted, nothing escapes the force of social construction, but alas, this social insight need not end or even exhaustively determine the terms of our conversations about such things as reproductive loss. Indeed, treating such loss and its complex dimensions as if they were simply harmful social products does violence to their integrity.

A TALE OF THE GRIEVING SELF

Having made these general comments about reproductive loss, let me now move to the heart of my project, to explore what I believe to be central features of this grief.[14] Because I am interested in eventually exploring what this grief looks like within the drama of faith, what I offer in this section is itself a kind of drama—a drama of traumatic reproductive loss. It is an "inside look" at four images of self that haunt women who struggle with a trauma of this kind.

As Wendy and I dug into the dirt in her yard that morning, for the first time in several days Wendy felt that she was doing something she had control over. She felt like an agent whose intentional actions, even the simple action of turning

over mud, were controlled and had measurable consequences.
This momentary feeling of control and agency stood in stark
contrast to the radical loss of agency she experienced in the
midst of her miscarriage. As she told me,

> A woman like myself is accustomed to viewing my body
> and my creative powers as something I control. My body,
> myself. I grew up believing that I could choose the condi-
> tions of my sexuality and my reproductivity. I thought I
> had a so-called choice. And yet now, I find myself walking
> around my kitchen bleeding away a life that I quite inten-
> tionally chose to make, . . . and I am completely powerless
> to save it. I am completely helpless in the face of what-
> ever it is nature appears to be doing here. I cannot stop the
> blood, Serene. It keeps pouring out of me and then washing
> away, lost. I cannot stanch its flow; it seeps out through the
> pores of my will which so ardently fights to stop it. I can-
> not change these things, even though I desire to do so more
> than anything else I have ever desired.

Wendy also explained that stealthily wrapped around this
sense of lost agency was its counterpart: a sense of enormous
guilt and responsibility for this miscarriage she could not stop
from happening. I hear this often when women speak of their
grief. Like Wendy, they tell me, again and again, that their first
thought when learning of their loss is that it somehow is their
fault. "What did I do to make this happen?" they ask. "Was
it that cigarette I smoked last Saturday? The glass of wine I
had three weeks ago? Did I not take the right vitamins?" Or
even more painfully, "Have I done something to deserve this?
Is God punishing me? Is this fate's revenge for sins I have committed in the past? Is it because of the abortion I had ten years
ago? Is it the drugs I used as a youth? Is it the mixed feelings
I had about the pregnancy in the first place?" Although most
women are able to recognize the often irrational quality of their
assumed guilt (as well as the level of responsibility they might
rightly assume), this does not lessen the insidious force of these
feelings. And these feelings are only exacerbated by a growing

medical rhetoric that holds women singularly responsible for the success or failure of their pregnancies. In such a context, a sense of culpability usually grows as women try to determine what happened medically; quite often, their past begins to look like one long tale of bad decisions and lost chances.[15]

Tied up with this first feature of reproductive grief—the paradoxical intertwining of lost agency and guilt—is a second feature that marks one's sense of self: the enormous sense of a future lost, a hope forever deferred. Regardless of how one medically views the status of tissue produced by the pregnancy, the woman who wants a pregnancy is going to imagine the potential life that is at stake in every attempt at pregnancy. Further, she does not imagine it as just any life; she views it as a particular life, the life of her potential child. She immediately envisions it as a person with a smile like her father's, or thick black hair like her sister's. She also begins to measure her own future in terms of this imagined child's development. She imagines where he, her son, will sleep or what she, her daughter, will wear. She envisions him at school or her learning to drive. She conjures up the many possible tones of his voice or the shape of her feet, at birth and then at fifty. The woman's body begins to anticipate holding the child; she can smell her daughter's birthday cake; she can hear her son singing in his high school years. Her whole being, it seems, stretches itself into this child's future, and this future becomes the space of her own becoming. In the words of Paul Tillich, "All time is expectation." For her, this could not be truer, for she is quite literally expecting this child. And then, her hope dies.

When a desired pregnancy fails—whether it is through a stillbirth or a failed in vitro fertilization—the woman experiences this known and yet unknown child not just as "failing" but also as "dying." And with it dies a passionately imagined future, a future that is both the child's and the woman's. She thus grieves not only an immediate loss, but also the loss of an entire lifetime, a lifetime lived vividly in the drama of her hoping. In many cases, this effects a peculiar and painful twist on a woman's relation to time itself. As the future she imagines collapses, so too collapses her capacity to envision the future with any sense of expectancy. In this sense, the death of expectation harshly reconfigures her understanding of time. Women have told me that along with their inability to make a child comes a sense of their inability to make a future. When this happens, time stretches before them as a story of parching barrenness or violent bloodiness; in either case, it no longer stretches before them as a book that they are invited to write. As Wendy described it, she spent days, perhaps even months— she couldn't measure it—wandering in a strange land where time held no promise. Out of kilter, disoriented, bleeding, her body could not anticipate with joy even the next second of its existence, to say nothing of the years of future existence she had previously celebrated. Because the child that dies exists so completely in the space of hope and imagination, its death produces in the self its negative mirror image: the death of hope and of the capacity to relate to time as the space of expectancy, a welcoming space into which the self is invited to walk.[16]

This undoing of time finds its spatial counterpart in a woman's experience of the loss of bodily integrity. I call this third feature "the rupturing of self." It describes the confusion about self that occurs when one experiences the radical dissolution of the bodily borders that, in ordinary time, give the self a sense of internal coherence. By "borders," I refer to those morphological lines that mark the difference between the outside and the inside of self. In the throes of reproductive loss, women often describe a feeling of not knowing where they physically end and where the outside world begins. This is because their insides are quite literally falling out. A woman may also find that with the loss of borders comes a loss of one's ability to contain anything, either physically or psychically; her womb will not hold the child because, she feels, it has lost the ability to keep inside what belongs inside and to keep out what should not be in. So, too, at a cognitive and emotional level, she becomes more broadly confused about who she is. She cannot even contain herself. Wendy described this well. She told me that she felt fragmented, dispersed, like she was leaking into the world. For the woman who is miscarrying or having a stillbirth, this fragmentation means leaving pieces of herself and another in rags, in toilets, in medical waste cans; she tries to hold this all together but cannot. For the woman who suffers infertility, this loss of bodily integrity is often the result of the constant invasion of her body by medical technologies that promise to extend her reproductive powers. She becomes confused about where she ends and it begins. It becomes her, and vice versa. This dissolution also happens to her each time she sees the unwanted blood of her cycle, a blood whose cramping flow once again announces the advent of a dying, not a living.

This sense of not being able to contain life, of being fragmented and rupturing, is heightened even further as she begins to experience the fourth and perhaps most wrenching dimension of her grief: Her body becomes to her "the space of death." Several women have described this to me: "My womb is a deathbed, my body a grave." There is no other experience, in the mix of our many human griefs, that comes close to mirroring this. She carries death within her body, . . . but she does not die. Death becomes her. It fills her, a final death, and yet she lives to remember not a death diverted but a death accomplished and completed in her loins. The experience of stillbirth shows this most vividly. She holds in her womb the dead, imagined person whose future she has conjured. What does it mean to know one's self as a walking site of death itself? To have death quite literally inside you? It is hard to imagine the contours of this self—the self who is meant to produce, be creative, give life, and make a future, but who rather holds the stench of decay in the depths of her being, and she lives to tell of it. It is at this point in the experience of reproductive loss that women describe losing the capacity to speak. Instead, they wail or sit in aphasic silence. I believe this is partially because in Western culture, we have no images for the self who carries death within her. And because of this, we greet the woman who knows such loss with silence.[17]

If she is lucky, her imagination stops here, with death inside her. For many women, however, this imagery runs more deeply

and cuts more harshly as she begins to see herself not only as a
grave where death is held, but also as the active agent of that
dying. As Wendy described her grief that morning, she told me
she felt as if she had killed the life within her, that her body had
attacked and destroyed it. She asked me, then, what it meant
that her body, her womb, had *killed* the tissue and hopes we
were burying. Had her body murdered? Why had her body
rejected and killed the "other" whose life she so passionately
desired to nurture? While she knew she was speaking to me
in metaphors—she knew she had not intentionally destroyed
life—this murderous image had a profound grip upon her. Why
had she destroyed the other who lived inside her? she asked.
And why was she left alive to experience its dying? For a woman
raised to value maternal care, the ethical force of this experience of "killing the other" is devastating. Can one envision a
more powerfully antimaternal image? Not only does she not
give life as a mother should; her body also takes life away. Here
our most treasured conceptions of selfhood crack open and fall
apart, unable to bear the weight of this brutal possibility. And
again, those who suffer it are left without consoling images.

What I have offered here is a series of four very difficult
images that I believe capture something of the crisis this experience produces in the women who go through it. At many
different levels, these images of reproductive grief run counter
to our dominant conceptions of what persons are and do. In
doing so, these images form an aesthetic logic of selfhood that
runs counter to our culture's more familiar logics of selfhood.
(1) Instead of experiencing herself as an agent, the woman
grieving reproductive loss knows herself as powerless to stop it
and yet guilty for her perceived failure. (2) As her hope dies, she
also becomes a self without a future. (3) She is a self whose borders are as fluid as the blood she cannot stanch, a self undone.
(4) And in the space of this undoing, she is the antimaternal
self who does not give life; she takes it away. She is the space
of total and finalized death, perhaps even a killer. And in the
uncanniest twist of all, she is the one who lives through this all:
she carries death and yet lives. When these four dimensions of

her loss are woven into a single picture of grief, we find a portrait of suffering that is painfully unique in its form. As such,
it is a suffering that calls out to feminists and theologians: Can
your visions of the self hold me? Can your theory bear my
weight? To this call, let us now turn.

THREE FEMINIST TALES OF THE SELF

Can feminist theory bear the weight of this experience and the
portrait of selfhood it gives us? One would like to think that it
could. But that morning in the rain, Wendy and I felt otherwise. We simply could not find a feminist language to hold it.
What I suggest here is that part of the reason we failed to do so
is that feminist theories of the self are, for the most part, predi-
cated upon scripts of personhood that not only do not include
the possibility of reproductive loss; they also run counter to it.[18]
To illustrate this, let us look briefly at the three central "tales of
the self" that feminists have used to theorize women's experience in general and reproduction in particular: the tale of the
self as "agent," as "maternal ground," and as "discursive site."

Consider the first account of the self: *the self as agent.* It
is one that North American public discourse rehearses frequently. It undergirds the principal legal arguments given by
liberal feminists for reproductive freedom as well as a myriad
of other political issues related to women's emancipation.[19] In
this story, woman is figured principally as a self who, following
the logic of classical social contract theory, is endowed with an
indissoluble right to self-determination. Central to the enactment of this freedom is her natural ownership of her body. She
is a "choosing agent" who possesses a "productive body." She is
the self who is always in the process of becoming her own "self-
creation" as she makes the world she desires for herself.

While feminist theorists have strong grounds for critiquing
this model of the self, even the harshest feminist critics of this
model are reluctant to sacrifice agency and self-determination
in their bid to dismantle the false foundations of liberalism. I

share this reluctance but remain troubled by the forms of self this construction excludes. When a morphology of reproductive loss is taken as the context for conceptualizing selfhood, the language of choice falls apart because the self is figured as having thwarted agency—thwarted capacity for self-creation. While the self may still possess its body, the body refuses to yield what the self desires. Nowhere is this tension between the liberal agential self and the self of reproductive loss more obvious than in contrasting accounts of abortion and miscarriage. In the first case, feminist theory narrates a scenario in which a woman's right to self-determination significantly guides the process of moral reflection; in the second, the same biological event demands an acknowledgment of the profound limits of that self-determining power. In other words, the first self presents herself as agent; the second experiences herself as radically nonagential. However, because the nonagential self stands in imagistic tension with the first, it unfortunately remains not only untheorized but also unacknowledged.

The second account of the self finds its subtext not in the language of rights and principles, but in the dramatically different world of feminist reflections on *"care" and "relationality."*[20] According to this model, the self is understood principally in terms of her (socialized) capacity for being aware of and attending to the particular (not universal) needs of others. Rather than emphasizing the rigid boundaries of the self-possessed self, this self is relationally more fluid. Her self comes into being through the play of her interactions with those around her. Although most of the literature on care is careful to avoid essentializing this characteristic of women's identity, it is clear that undergirding the construction of this self is a set of strong assumptions about the logic of maternity; it is at heart a discourse about motherhood and nurturing insofar as it draws on a morphology of reproductive care to fund its image of the self. The self is thus figured principally as the embodied site of relational engagement. She exists in the play of her responses to particularized otherness. She is the space of maternal origin.[21]

While feminists have gained much political ground through the assertion of this second model of the self, particularly with respect to the unique insights that women's socialized experience can bring to theory, its limits with respect to an aesthetic of reproductive loss should be obvious. Instead of giving us a self whose relational connection to the other is life giving and formative, infertility, miscarriage, and stillbirth suggest the form of a self who has failed to embody the logic of maternity: the story of a self as an embodied site marked by its inability to care (in a very profound sense) for the other. Her body is a place where nature is in decline, where death dwells, where the telos of maternity is radically denied. Morphologically, this woman's story thus runs counter to the maternal myth undergirding this dimension of contemporary theory. She is the barren womb, the negated self. She refuses the logic of origins and repels the so-called psychoanalytic nostalgia for the space of undifferentiated unity.

The third, well-known account of the self in feminist theory is rooted in the post-structuralist rendering of *the destabilized "subject."*[22] The self posited in this story is not so much a coherent self as a constantly shifting site wherein multiple discourses and social forces converge, reconfigure, fragment, and diverge. Neither her agency nor her body serves to limit her. Post-structuralist feminism thus offers the story of the self undone, the ruptured subject, the person strewn into the chaotic coursings of history. One could even call this self the "unnarrative" woman. She resists any attempt to locate her identity in the stability presupposed by narrative assumptions about time and space.

Again, feminist theory has in recent years gained much political ground through the introduction of this particular account of the self. These gains have been most evident in the strident rejection of the feminist essentialisms that haunt both the rights and care models of the self. This account of the self breaks up narrative and allows for the radical differences marking women's lives to surface. These gains, however, do not temper its potential difficulty in dealing with the story of reproductive loss.

Unlike the other two accounts, which negate the logic of reproductive loss, this story risks inappropriately valorizing tropes of
rupturing, fragmenting, "coming undone." For a woman like
Wendy, who was bleeding for days, a theory that hemorrhages
the self, can hardly be consoling. For one whose very body is
being strewn into history, buried in earth, images of the post-
structuralist boundless self hardly come as a comfort.

In light of the dramatic failure of these three tales of the
self to address issues pertinent to reproductive loss, what am
I suggesting that feminist theory do? For one, I do not think
that feminist theory should give up on these tales. Each has
served (and continues to serve) important political functions in
the women's movement and crucial pastoral functions in the
lives of individual women. It thus seems to me that we need
to add yet another tale to the mix of our stories of the self, the
aesthetic drama of the self suggested by reproductive loss: the
nonagential, hopeless, fragmenting, death-carrying self I have
just described. What it will mean for her story to enter the stage
of feminist theory, I am not yet certain, . . . for contemporary
theory on the whole has a difficult time incorporating tales of
loss and mourning.[23] And the tale I tell here, in its particularity, raises questions about the nature of the self that are much
larger than the particular story, . . . and hence incorporating
it will push feminist theories of the self in substantive ways I
have only hinted at here. One thing I am certain of, however, is
that the Christian tradition does have resources imagining this
self, . . . and perhaps it is here that feminist theory might find
insights that help to move forward on this.

DEATH IN THE TRINITY:
ANOTHER STORY OF THE SELF

Having laid out these feminist scripts of selfhood and the challenges that reproductive loss raises for each, let me now turn
to the area of constructive doctrine and ask the question: How
might feminist theology speak to traumatic experiences such

as Wendy's? How might we construct doctrinal spaces that include such lived realities?

Because my theological work is most significantly informed by my own Reformed heritage, I turn to this tradition as a source for such reflections. The first question that arises here is this: Where might we best anchor this topic? What doctrinal locus might best hold and shape the unique characteristics of this grieving? One answer that immediately comes to mind (an answer that is not very Reformed) is that we should turn our thoughts to Mary, the mother of Jesus. After all, feminists have long turned to her as a source for creative insight into the place of the feminine and the maternal in the divine economy. Why not engage her figure in reflections on reproductive loss as well?

Such a turn, I have discovered, is not helpful because feminist work on Mary has fallen prey to many of the same problems I just outlined in feminist theory. Several dominant themes arise in feminist accounts of her: (1) Mary as womb, productive ground, the mother of God; (2) Mary as choosing agent, the one who, in the Magnificat, "chooses" God (the Mary of liberation theology); and (3) Mary as the site of fragmenting discourse (the Mary of Julia Kristeva's essay "Stabat Mater").[24] In each of these accounts of Mary, one finds contemporary feminists attempting to retrieve her as a site of emancipatory discourse for women; but they do so in a manner that recapitulates some of the limits I have just outlined. In other words, none of the theological renderings of Mary morphologically resonates with the economy of Wendy's reproductive loss. (At this point, there is a temptation to turn to Mary as the mother of the Jesus who died on the cross, the mother who experiences maternal loss in his crucifixion. Such a turn, however, fails because in instances of child death, the mother's barrenness and her bodily disintegration are not at issue.)

Having said this, we are still left with the question of where to turn, doctrinally, for resources that might aesthetically respond to this experience of reproductive loss in meaningful ways. Several doctrines central to the Reformed tradition quickly suggest themselves: creation, sin, and eschatology. Creation, it seems, might be a good place to start because it would allow us to reflect upon concepts like finitude and providence. In this context, one could explore the Christian affirmation that although these losses are painful, they may well be the body's own wonderful way of dealing with pregnancies that are not biologically tenable. One could also explore the faith affirmation that because time is a gift of God, forever unfolding in God's mysterious promise, we as Christians should be aware that we do not control the future, that time is not ours, and that the dashed hopes of pregnancies lost were hopes that stretched beyond the bounds of our control. It strikes me, however, that while these themes are important, they would not be well received by a woman in the midst of the grief I have described. She does not want to hear that her loss is just nature "doing its thing," nor does she need a sermon on the excesses of her hope.

One could also anchor one's reflections on this grief in the doctrine of sin. Anchored here, one could wax eloquent about the various sinful social structures that create the oppressive conditions causing this grief to occur in the first place. Here, one could explore the ways sexism, classism, and especially racism and the abuse of the environment contribute to reproductive loss. But it strikes me that this locus fails to address the dimensions of reproductive loss that cannot finally be reduced to human culpability or characterized as oppression. The option of eschatology also looks promising because, in the context of this doctrine, one could look more carefully at the nature of Christian hope and explore the place held by these events in the economy of ultimate redemption. One could explore, for instance, both the problems and the promise that attend women's common belief that in heaven, these lost imagined lives are held tenderly. While there is certainly much to be said on this topic, I think that eschatology has often been used (wrongly so) as a facile palliative for those who mourn; and as such, it presents challenges of its own. For example, is it faithful or even helpful for infertile women to imagine that they have children in heaven?

As these comments on doctrine suggest, I believe it is important to consider the audience to whom one is speaking when one does constructive theological reflection—an insight that, incidentally, I learned most convincingly from John Calvin.[25] In this regard, the doctrines above are not appropriate starting points for this project because their forms—the dramatic structures that drive them—do not rhetorically benefit (even though they might be quite true) the context I am addressing here: women whose conception of self has been devastated by reproductive loss. As I argued earlier, these women have told me that what they need first and foremost in their grief is an image that can hold their experience. As Wendy described it, she sought a vision of divinity into which she could crawl and then rest.[26] What she sought, I believe, was a theological form that might allow her to imagine "God with her" as she struggled with lost agency, dashed hopes, disintegrating boundaries, and a body that carries death. I also believe that within this image, she hoped to find at least a whisper of the grace that would heal her.

An image of God "standing with" (or perhaps "stooping and digging in the rain with") the woman ravaged by grief at the loss of her hoped-for children: Where does one turn to find this? Let me make a rather unusual suggestion by pointing us toward the doctrine of the Trinity, a doctrine that, in the Reformed tradition, has been revitalized by the work of Karl Barth and his Lutheran student, Jürgen Moltmann. I believe it is a doctrine that, when informed by the particular character of reproductive loss, offers us—if only sketchily—a theological way into the complex of issues I have been exploring.

To begin this exploration, let me offer, in rough outline, the principal features of the doctrine of the Trinity I am working with here: a view of the Trinity that follows a rather classical logic. At the heart of this doctrine of God is the classical affirmation that the God of the Christian faith is a trinity of persons in perichoretic relation: a community of mutually indwelling persons (persons both distinct and unified). This community-of-persons-as-One-God exists eternally in a dance of relating where each offers freely to the other the fullness of its love and receives back from the other the same; each thus exists fully and freely for the sake of the other and in the other. Out of this Trinitarian community is born creation, that "other" which God creates in freedom, for the sheer sake of loving it, for the sheer sake of sharing with it this abounding Trinitarian love. This creation, in turn, is given the possibility of knowing itself as God's beloved and, in faith, offering praise to the Trinitarian God who has elected it for such glory. These beloved human creatures of God, for reasons eternally unfathomable, choose not to know this glory but to live in sin; they choose the impossible possibility. Though this sinful choice does not have the power to banish God's love from the world, God laments the creature's loss and hence its disoriented wandering in a falsely constructed world where grace is unknown.

The story goes on. The Trinitarian God, who eternally loves this world, comes into this world as a person, to walk among these beloved, fallen creatures. This coming is the most fully outworking of a love that has eternally sought to be "for the other," to love the other unconditionally. Met by sin, however, this one who comes, Jesus Christ, is hung upon a cross to die. What happens when this one who exists eternally in the Godhead and yet occupies our humanness dies a very human death? God refuses to turn from us, even in the most brutal grip of tortured death and divine abandonment, and instead takes death into Godself. In doing so, the judge judged in our place enacts yet again the reality of the creature's redemption. What is this redemption? It is the reality that not even death on a cross can cause God to withdraw God's love from those whom God has elected. On the day of resurrection, the redemptive power of the cross is confirmed as the redemption of God.

How might this story speak to women suffering from reproductive loss? At one level, it points to the reality of God's redemptive love for creation; it is a love that extends to all persons, including women suffering from reproductive loss, and it is a love that all are invited to know, even the women who grieve deeply. In addition to this, however, I believe this classical version of the Trinity (if pushed in a particular way) also allows us to see something about God's solidarity with women grieving reproductive loss *specifically*. In contemporary as well as classical discussions of the Trinity, theologians have been hard-pressed to give an account of what happens in the Godhead when Christ, a part of this Godhead, dies. What transpires in the Godhead when one of its members bleeds away? Theologians like Moltmann and Luther have urged us to affirm that on the cross, God takes this death into the depths of Godself.[27] The Trinity thus holds this death. The first person holds the second, who undergoes death, united with the second by the power of the Spirit. But how can the living Godhead hold death within it? The tradition has told us that at this point in the story, our language breaks down, and we must simply ponder the cross and its mysteries.

Perhaps the tradition is right, but perhaps its imaginative resources have been limited by the morphological imaginations of its mostly male theologians. Perhaps what we find in this space of silence is the image of the woman who, in the grips of a stillbirth, has death inside her and yet does not die. Consider the power of this as an image for the Trinity. When Christ is crucified, God's own child dies. For the God who sent this child into the world bearing the hope of God's eternal love, this death is a death of hope, the hope that the people who see this child will believe. It is the death of a possibility that has never been, the possibility of true human community. Further, because the God who bears this loss will not turn away from God's people, God is in a sense rendered helpless in the face of this dying. God cannot stop it; and yet by letting it happen, God also bears guilt for it. In this dying, the borders of divine identity are also confused and made fluid as the One who is the source of life eternal bears now the stamp of complete, full death. In death, Christ's divine and human natures are transposed with riveting force. And perhaps most wrenching, this is a death that happens deep within God, not outside of God but in the very heart—perhaps the womb—of God. It is a death that consumes God, that God holds, making a grave of the Trinity. And yet, like the women we have heard from in my stories, this death-bearing grave of a God paradoxically does not die but lives. And She lives to love yet again and to offer to the world the gift of the future.

How might this vision of the Trinity unfold in the imaginations of women who suffer reproductive loss? First, this is not an image that should encourage women to imagine their own suffering as redemptive. They are not God, and even for God, the suffering itself is not the source of our redemption; the persistence of love in the midst of suffering is that redemptive source. Thus, the poetic move here is not to identify these women with God or vice versa, but rather to suggest a morphological space within which they might imagine God's solidarity with them as those who lose a future they had hoped for and who carry the weight of this loss inside themselves. As an image of God with them, this rupturing, antimaternal tale of the Trinity won't stop their sorrow, but it might lessen their sense of isolation, which is no small step in the process of healing. Even more important, if a woman can imagine this God with her, then perhaps she can glimpse the resurrection and remember that, although she may have wanted to die, she did not die. And in her continued life, the future presses upon her gently. It waits for her now and will wait for her as long as she takes.

As I ponder this image of the miscarrying, stillbirthing, barren-wombed God, I imagine Her stooping with Wendy and me in the garden that morning—no, I imagine Her holding Wendy, curling Her own ruptured body around Wendy's, and rocking her. "I know," She says. "I know." And I imagine Wendy finding great solace in her solidarity with this God who has born such loss, . . . with her sense of utter aloneness melting away. I also imagine Wendy looking at God and being even more amazed and comforted by the differences between herself and this God who holds her. Both of them grieve the loss not only of a child but also of an entire world. But in the depths of this loss, God—unlike Wendy—has the power to save her, the power to love her, passionately, deeply, the power to redeem a child like Wendy, who is not of God's loins but, as the Trinity curls around her, is bonded to God by a grace that is sheer gift.

So what does this redemption mean in Wendy's case? We have the resurrection after three days in the grave, the future that presses upon her—and we have mystery.

In closing I should comment that there is more work to be done on this image of the Trinity than I can do here. Feminist theologians have already taken some strides in this direction by offering the image of the woman-with-child as an analogy for perichoretic indwelling. What these discussions miss, however, is the reality of the cross, the reality of stillbirth, infertility, and miscarriage. What they therefore miss is a rather ironic fact: the image that most effectively captures the nature of God's redeeming grace is not an image of mothering, but an image of maternal loss. It seems to me that this antimaternal narrative holds great possibilities for feminists interested in reconceptualizing the nature of both the self and community. In its relinquishment of naturalized social bonding, it opens space for us to imagine new forms of relating, forms that take their cues from the always gifted economy of grace and not the ever-producing maternal ground. And finally, this antimaternal image is the act of imagining new narratives that enable the return of a future and the possibility of grace to take hold of those traumatized by loss.

9

Mourning and Wonder

Love comes to you.

There are scenes in the Gospel stories that are so familiar to me I sometimes forget they are scenes at all. The story line simply blends into the comings and goings of my day. Like a childhood jingle, they hum along in the background, giving everything pace and color. Sometimes I completely forget them, just like the existence of air or gravity. That is, until something jolts me into awareness, like having no air underwater or watching the ground rush forward on a roller-coaster ride. Suddenly, there they are in full view—startling little facts of life shouting out for attention.

So it is with the sin-grace story that hums along in my own and in most Christian imaginations. It's a tale so common that most people never pause to think about it, until suddenly one day it's not there—and gasping for breath, you start frantically looking around for it, . . . and if you're lucky enough to find it, like air, its utter peculiarity knocks you flat again.

For me, that gasping started almost ten years ago, prompted by a series of events that left my faith hurling downward and led to the writing of this book. It didn't happen suddenly but was nudged forward first by my midlife grappling with hard but not unusual life events—the loss of a pregnancy, the collapse of my marriage, a sudden and then long illness, the death of a friend— and then pushed ahead full throttle by a few monumental events—family members hit by the Oklahoma City bomb, my daughter almost dying in my arms, a brutal cancer, and a profound betrayal. It grew in intensity until one day I woke up and realized I could no longer rely on the oxygen that the sin-grace story had provided me for so many years. I had lost my faith.

In many ways, the essays in this book chronicle my search for that sin-grace story and the faith that went with it. They trace my desire to find a pathway back to a way of believing that might once again sustain me. In the throes of that search, I found the literature on trauma enormously helpful, partly because it introduced to me the insights of psychoanalysis and the social sciences on violence, and partly because it tied my own traumatic struggles to similar struggles undergone by friends, students, neighbors, and most important, the masses of severely traumatized people around the world. Most of the time my own trials paled in comparison to what I witnessed (as soon as I was willing to see), but the literature on trauma, at its finely honed best, did me the great favor of keeping the line between everyday existence and traumatic pathology thin enough to foster honesty and connection with those whose suffering far exceeded my own.

What is theologically interesting about this journey is that when I finally got hold of the sin-grace story I thought I had lost, it was a new, revised version that filled my lungs with air again. In the process of tromping myself intellectually and emotionally through the world of trauma literature as well as through my own shifting interior landscape, a change transpired in my theology that was as profound as it was hard to see, at least while it was happening. To see this change, it's helpful to compare it to the story that previously inflated my faith.

SIN AND GRACE

The basic plot line is rather simple. Most Christians know it by heart. God creates the world. The world gets into trouble and can't get out of it. God, out of love, dramatically intervenes so as to save the world—Jesus comes, dies, is raised—and as a result, something new and good emerges. Humanity is saved. Sin is met by grace, and grace conquers it. In this regard, it is fundamentally the tale of a triumphant vanquishing in which, at the end of the day, grace abounds.

In traditional Christian language, that harm is called "sin," and its forms are as myriad as the experiences that comprise history itself, a topic discussed more fully in chapter 7. Every generation is given the task of renaming it and grappling afresh with the strange Christian insistence that sin is both social and personal and that we are both its perpetrators and its victims. In terms of grace, the tradition has similarly strange insistence, also traced in chapter 7. Whatever one says about grace, this "healing good" that comes from God arrives upon the scene of sin freely and unbidden, as a gift that descends and heals without having been earned or won. It appears without warrant. That is what makes it grace. It cannot be bought or achieved by those who need it.

Over the centuries, this basic story line has burrowed into almost every nook and cranny of church faith and practice and inhabits many corners of North American nonreligious cultural life as well. It pops up all over the Bible, be it in sagalike tales of God's Red Sea liberation of Israel or in Davidic poetry about lost sheep and good shepherds. It runs through worship services, humming through hymns, ringing out in the confession of sin and forgiveness, circling around the communion table, blurting itself out in benedictions. It's a story that also repeats itself in the theological writings of ecclesial teachers whose job it has been to examine it. Granted, there have been different accounts of what the problem is, what kind of dramatic action God takes in response to it, and how active human beings are in what transpires. Several of these have been explored in previous chapters. But running through them all—from medieval atonement theory to womanist survival theology—is a shared narrative, dramatic structure: God breaks in and saves. Whatever the problem might be—pride, lust, greed, unfaithfulness, social injustice—grace overwhelms it and something new happens.

That's the core moment, the heart of the story: a takeover action wipes the slate clean and starts things anew.

As with most enduring stories, this is a tale that pulses not only through minds but also through bodies. For those who learn the story in church school and then breathe it night and day, as I did, this redemptive dynamic unfolds in the motions of one's physical gestures—determining how a person feels in one's own skin—just as it patterns the deep logic of streaming desires, the conscious longings as well as those unknown but insistent and real. The gestures it patterns are actually so deeply embedded in thought and bodily processes that one often fails to realize that they are being enacted. When I have an argument with a friend, for example, my almost instinctual response is to start trying to figure out what went wrong and then to start looking around for what will fix it, the intervention that will save us. I seldom think, explicitly, oh, well, Jesus or God or the Trinity will fix it—but deep inside my brain stem somewhere, the hope that a transcendent God will make it right springs eternal, particularly when I've run out of my own ideas as to how I might make it right. Expecting the world to be broken and expecting grace to come—it is the air and gravity of sin-grace imagination. That's what makes Christians such inveterate hopers. In our minds, something is always about to happen. And then it does.

FAILURE AND PRESENCE

For most of my life, it never occurred to me that there might be a problem with this central scene. This didn't mean that I had an uncritical assessment of the tradition. My work in classical and Reformation theology as well as in feminist thought and postcolonial theory has long been committed to exposing hidden dangers in certain versions of this tale. For the most part, however, this involved tinkering around the edges of the sin-grace story, rearranging things here and there, changing an ending or two, asking provoking questions now and then, even daring to say we should rethink what sin is and reconsider what God's saving action looks like. Nonetheless, throughout it all, the fundamental dramatic structure of the sin-grace model remained unquestioned. I believed, in ways as unconscious as they were articulated, that the universe itself was unceasingly arranged according to the inner order of sin-grace.

Then things began to shift. The deeper I wandered into the reality of traumatic violence, the more difficult the story was to bear, for several reasons. First, time and again I found that whether it was liberation theology, feminist theology, or substitutionary atonement theology (all of which rely on a version of the basic story line), the story bred an almost instinctual optimism about change that is hard to sustain. At the crudest level, it trains one to assume that if one works hard enough at healing, one will obtain what one asks for. Social structures can be mended by justice-seeking policies. Life can become more ordered by getting one's head on straight and learning to believe in oneself. And so on.

This optimism, while existentially helpful when it comes to responding to some forms of harm and healing, fails to account for the harsh fact that the vast majority of trauma survivors reach the end of their lives still caught in its terrifying grip. Leah may never find the love she seeks; that hole in her may be too vast and wide to ever be filled. Latisha and Rachel may never sleep a full night because the harms they have suffered reach so deep into their bodies and minds that hope simply cannot find it. And the list goes on. If imagination is the place in which grace meets sin, as I've argued throughout this book, then how do we come to grips with the fact that a mind disordered and diseased by violence might well be one in which the very "imagining" mechanism necessary for redemption has been broken . . . beyond repair. It is a hard truth, and it raises tough questions about trauma's "solvability" and the scope of grace's saving power—at least in terms of the sin-grace narrative structure.

A second concern complicates matters more. For those who are able to actually move forward and experience some degree of healing from traumatically inflicted harms, it seldom happens in a direct, linear manner, and the past from which they are recovering never completely leaves them; it is never vanquished. This means that in lived experience, most survivors are never completely made anew and thereby miraculously restored to the self they were before harm found them. More realistically, the old gouges of violence in the brain and body are carried forward with them, albeit in a more manageable form. Recall John, the Vietnam vet's words in chapter 2, who says of his own nostalgic yearning to be healed by returning to a purer, before-trauma self: "The way forward is never straight, and there is no going back. Having lived in the land of the bizarre, all one can do is step forward into a future where that bizarre world continues to haunt you, but perhaps in a new way. A space is opened up for other kinds of knowing as well. But the two worlds continue to haunt one another."[1] In light of this reality, the challenge is to think grace in ways that do not require pure outcomes or an impossible, radical newness.

A third discomfort grew as well, perhaps the most complex one. At the heart of the sin-grace story is the claim that because sin's hold upon us is total and inescapable and because the grace that God bestows is unmerited, gifted, and free, the only way we finally know grace is by virtue of a dramatic outside intervention which surprises us, shocks us, pulls us up short, and turns us around. The images used to capture this relation between sin and grace are often quite violent because the imagined relation is one of radical discontinuity and divinely established relation. As Karl Barth described it, the rock of revelation is thrown at our heads, and bam—we receive new knowledge of a grace that saves. Dramatically, we undergo a psychic overwhelming, an epistemological undoing, a dismantling of sin's pretensions, and a rendering trivial of our usual protective mechanism. The difficulty with this dimension of the sin-grace story, from the perspective of trauma, is not hard to see. It replicates the experience of being battered, violated, and made helpless in the grasp of a more powerful force. Who on earth would want this God to heal you? And yet, when viewed from the perspective of trauma theory, it is not easy to imagine an alternative. Like sin, the hold of traumatic violence on the psyche can often be total, and as therapeutic models insist, an outside intervention is quite frequently required. How does one experience the radical new-ness of grace and of healing hope without simultaneously being ravaged by the demands it places upon you?

As I wrestled with these gut-felt limits to the sin-grace story, the sturdy ground under my faith feet began to slowly dissolve, not in grand or immediately noticeable ways but in ways more subtle and enduring. It began to simply not make sense. Grace needed to be larger than the lives of those who never recovered. It needed also to be sturdier than a tale of a straightforward recovery, less sanguine, less optimistically naive, more scrappy and ambiguous. It needed as well to be imaged as gentle and embracing while not losing its radical otherness and its refresh-ing newness.

THE BODY'S GRACE

Finding such a trauma-wizened version of the sin-grace story was not easy, however. I looked high and low for it, wander-ing around in other religions and other cultural views of gifts and love. Like Augustine scrambling after truth, I chewed up worlds of thought in search of food that would satisfy. I even returned to the most theologically familiar place I knew, the cross, and tried looking at it with freshly faithless eyes. Turning it this way and that, I hoped to find some splendid secret I had accidently missed in my more pious days.

In the end, however, the search yielded nothing. When it came to other religions, the existential grip I needed was miss-ing—revealing just how Christian my un-Christianess was. When it came to the cross, I fared no better. Instead of a splen-did secret, I was left with a messy pile of conflicted feelings. Its brutality never failed to provoke deep sadness, a harsh reminder of the violence we are capable of inflicting. At the same time, its gruesomeness never completely turned my head away. Instead, each time I looked, I found myself restlessly transfixed before it, both bewildered and fascinated by its oddity. What a strange mix; it was sadly depressing while still enchanting. It pulled downward while startling attention up and outward. Grief and surprise—an interesting combination of reactions, yes, but hardly the new account of grace that I was looking for.

Or so I thought, until other, less thought-centered processes began to unfold in my life. Following the advice of a friend, I took up a new set of physical practices. I was intrigued by what trauma clinicians tell us about the visceral traces left behind by traumatic events, traces like quick-startle responses, headaches, exhaustion, muscle aches, distractibility, and depression—all of which sporadically haunted my own interior world. If the aftermath of violence was this visceral, I reasoned, it made sense that grace capable of touching it should be equally physical.

Working with a local Chinese doctor, I began acupuncture treatments combined with strong-tasting teas and simple massages. I also signed up for yoga classes at the community center and started stretching and breathing. As my body relaxed into the rhythms of both practices—my "liturgies of flesh," as I called them—I began to notice changes in my tactile and emotional responses to events and people. Over the next five years, this shift continued to deepen and expand, and it continues still. Along with it has come the slow rediscovery of the sin-grace story I'd lost.

How can I describe this physical version? I often thought about these newly experienced "body-stories" in the terms familiar to "trauma and grace." Broadly speaking, it had a three-part dramatic structure. When strung together, they tell a single story, much like the Emmaus tale or Calvin's three-staged liturgy of psalm singing, albeit a visceral version. If the parts are superimposed, however, they form a holographic image more like the overlapping stories from the women's self-defense class or the juxtaposed accounts of Mary and Rachel's wrestling with the death of their children, but in this instance, told through the text of muscle and nerves rather than Scripture and story.

The body-story goes like this:

The physical action that initiates both practices is a *disruptive* encounter with an "other" that is both welcomed and disturbing. In the case of acupuncture, it's the prick of a needle guided by the doctor's hand. With yoga, it is the first big intake of air. In both instances, this external presence—a needle, air, hands, a voice . . . —bears upon the body by breaking open and traversing normal physical boundaries. Be it a boundary of skin or muscle or lung space, this presence crosses over the edge of an accustomed world, overwhelming it "from beyond." It is often uncomfortable and can even hurt, despite the fact that it is harmless. It brings to awareness areas of tightness or pain that may have gone unnoticed or ignored for years. Your arm suddenly aches, your stomach jumps, your eyelid twitches. And in this way, the encounter pulls interiorized wounds into open, conscious space.

To use the language of trauma theory, the body offers up visceral testimony. Tactile memories are spoken, and tales of harm are physically dictated into bodily text, as you become aware of, let's say, a sharp pain that lingers from an old car wreck or ache of a jaw that's been clenched since childhood. It's a testimony initiated by an outside intervention that mirrors a traumatic and overwhelming event but enacts it differently because now it is wanted and safe. Cast theologically, this is a bodily feeling that replicates the drama of classical Christian accounts of how grace appears on our horizons. From a place beyond, grace comes toward us, disturbs us, traverses our boundaries, and dwells disruptively within us as it gives testimony to the previously unspoken sins/traumas that occupy us.

Another sensation then follows. At the very moment you are knocked off balance by the encounter, you discover—and this is remarkable—that you are supported and held steady by something unexpected. It is a *strange, unprecedented form of embrace.* The support might be an acupuncturist's hands, a yoga teacher's voice, a wall you rest your legs against, or a supportive community that you learn to lean on; it might even be a routinized prayer chant or an internal memory of your former

balance. Anything secure, strong, snuggly fit, and sturdy can do
the trick. What matters is the physical sensation of simultaneously loosing your self (to pain, to fear, or to just the strangeness
of the motion) and being safely held while it happens.

According to trauma theory, this off-kilter embrace enacts
the therapeutic insight: by testifying and bearing witness, you
intuitively learn to bear up under the weight of the trauma you
are speaking. You take the risk of speech, and your voice is held
by the witness; in the play of that process, you learn how to
hold yourself, how to bear up. Yet in this experience, a permanent steadiness does not come at the end of a process, resolv-
ing the tension. Healing, if it comes, happens in the midst of
things. Theologically, this strange embrace physically performs
the promise that through grace, we are found, forgiven, and
fortified by God. Or better, it performs the claim of Jesus and
Paul that we must lose ourselves to gain ourselves (Mark 8:35;
Gal. 2:19–20). An important feature is that in this two-sided
experience, wounds are not magically healed but are borne.
Unlike the vanquishing of sin in the old story of sin-grace, this
double motion of loss and support physically enacts the reality
of being a sinner and a saint, not in succession but both at the
same time. Fully, we are undone and yet also held together in
the strong grip of divine compassion.

Then comes the third surprising moment. At the same instant
that you are undone and held, you are *thrown wide open*. With
each breath and needle prick, the world around you and within
you becomes more spacious and boundlessly present to you.
In acupuncture, it happens slowly as your nerves realign and
your energy moves outward. With yoga, it is immediate. Deep
breathing fills your body with air and then empties, lightening
your weight and outwardly orienting your gaze. In the space of
this openness, the people around you gently slip into view, their
breath becomes audible, and you notice the color of the walls,
the smell of traffic fumes, the sweat on your back.

Like the "reconnecting" third stage of healing described in
trauma literature, breathing viscerally extends you toward your
surroundings, taking in the mundane dimensions of all that you

encounter, the ebb and flow of the everyday, the not-so-trau-
matic unfolding of life in its normal cadence. With this comes
a remastering of the lost art of standing calmly in the present.
Theologically cast, the moment enacts the embodied grace feeling of accepting your life as a gift and a promise, and living in
the expansive sense of time and space that this gift provides. In
full abundance, this grace strengthens the capacity to act at the
very same time it invites you to fuller love of neighbor and ever-
deepening love of the God who both frees and holds.

MOURNING AND WONDER

If imagination is comprised as much of flesh and heart as it is
of beliefs and well-formed ideas, then it follows that these practices eventually shifted my conscious theology of sin and grace.
Not surprisingly, the change came without much fanfare, stop-
ping short of a full-fledged conversion. It was significantly soul
shifting, nonetheless, because it cultivated in me two forms of
feeling-thought, or better, *two habits of spirit* that, when consciously accepted, rearranged my world.

Recall my encounter with the cross: sadness and startled
enchantment, despair coupled with restless surprise. Even
though I could not see it at the time, this strange pairing
expressed a deep truth about the riddle of "trauma and grace."
Cast in richer language than those initial raw emotions express,
they point to the larger experiences of *mourning and wonder*.
Mourning fully and wondering openly—at the end of this book,
this is what remains: the soul-response evoked by the cross. To
mourn and to wonder, that is what the spirit yearns for when it
stands in the midst of trauma and breathes in the truth of grace.
Mourning and wonder—neither one answers the question that
trauma poses to grace. They are, instead, states of mind that, if
nurtured, open us to the experience of God's coming into torn
flesh, and to love's arrival amid violent ruptures.

To explain this further, follow me into an imagined theater
of mind where mourning and wonder form the principal frame

of reference for every experience. It is a place where the gruesome, odd cross casts its shadow across a vast mental universe,
giving it order and direction.

Imagine that at the edge of every thought, every sensation,
the mind takes a backward glance and then a forward one.
Taking it all in, the mind then pauses cautiously and considers
the ever-darkening quality of what it beholds. The caution is
because the cross exposes how easily we are pulled into violent situations and how devastating are its effects upon us. The
ever-darkening aspect is because just as the cross never recedes
entirely from view, those gouges and tears never completely
vanish. More often than not, they persist and even grow, in
one form or another, making the mind's habits of hoping a
complex endeavor.

But hope is not impossible. What is surprising about this
forward and backward glance is that the very capacity to undertake these glancing motions announces the presence of both
surprise and possibility at the edge of every look. If the mind's
eye could behold all of it at once, no glance behind or ahead
would be necessary. There would be nothing to discover, nothing new to catch the eye. But this is not the case. This roving
mind's eye is implicitly curious, seduced by possibility, constantly gazing out *with interest*, even when its focus is off kilter, wrongly aimed, or narrowly turned inward. Every glance
seeks a world; every look is surrounded by the future, the next
moment, the space of seeing. This is the surprise, the enchantment that the cross evokes. The fact that the cross endures is
truth of grace itself: it is the fact that time marches forward,
and flesh persists in its unwieldy promise of yet another touch,
another feeling, another memory, a trauma, a hope.

Much depends on what we do with these dispositions
cultivated at the foot of the cross—persistent loss and even
more persistent endurance and surprise. When it comes to
our response to loss, possibilities range widely. On one side,
there are tricks of mind where loss is forthrightly rejected or
repressed. Loss manifests itself in addictions; the pleasures of
oblivion trump the harshness of loss. On the other side, the

mind turns loss into an object of relentless reflection. Some call it melancholia; others name it depression; trauma survivors do it well—obsessively trying and yet always failing to master the wound that has felled them.

Between the two lies mourning, a disposition in which your heart and mind give in to the loss and consent to dwell in the trauma with as much attention as can be mustered. It requires acknowledging how much was lost, how deeply it matters, how unstable the world has become in the aftermath, and how difficult it feels to be ever moving forward. It requires full-bodied grieving for what you've lost. Grief is hard, actually the hardest of all emotions and perhaps most intolerable because its demands are so excruciating. It requires a willingness to bear the unbearable. As mourning, it requires turning private agony into public, shared loss. If you can learn to truly mourn, then there is at least the possibility of moving on. Not because the wound is mending or traumatic scars suddenly vanish—although it is oftentimes true that life appears meaningful in new ways as the grip of trauma upon you lessens. The gift of mourning is that fully awakening to the depth of loss enables you to at least learn, perhaps for the first time, that you can hold the loss: you can bear terrors of heart and body and still see your way forward with eyes open.

And here's where wonder appears, slipping through the web-like cracks that mourning presses onto the surface of trauma's enclosed world. Wondering is the simple capacity to behold the world around you (and within you), to be awed by its mystery, to be made curious by its difference, and to marvel at its compelling form. Whether it's an old college friend, a blade of grass, a garbage truck, or a weapon of mass destruction—wonder is not limited to beauty. You can wonder at the ugly and the gruesome, like the cross, or a car wreck, or the blank face of an addicted trauma survivor. It does require, however, becoming vulnerable to the object you behold, being open to its texture, sound, taste, history, politics, and so forth. It rests in a willingness to truly greet the object you behold and to revel in its surprises. To do this requires a vivid sense of where you

end and the object begins, for who can wonder at an otherness that has not become other, lacking distinction from you
because you have no edge or ending?

In all these ways, wonder is the complete opposite of the
truncated, shut-down systems of perception that traumatic
violence breeds in its victims. Traumatic violence violates
bodily and psychic boundaries as it overwhelms and takes over
its victims. In contrast, to feel wonder when looking at the
face of your grandmother, or (better) the nameless mumbling
man sitting next to you on the bus, you must occupy a place
of self-conscious distance from them while also remaining
open enough to their peculiar features that you can marvel at
the oddity of their form. So, too, with the cross: to stand in
its shadow and behold it with wonder requires the confident
knowledge that the cross is not yours but Christ's, and yet you
remain and are utterly vulnerable to its mysteries and laid bare
by its witness.

The theological story of Eden's innocence and the fall captures this double play of mourning and wonder. We live in a
world where, if we are lucky, a gardenlike freshness greets us
on the edge of every forward and backward glance. Time opens
up in the splendor of unceasingly, insistent novelty. It was not,
now it is, and then it's gone. This feature of our lives—the ever-
present given and the press of an unknown future—makes us
all, in every Edenic moment, newly innocent creatures.

And yet, into this temporally insistent Eden comes the fall—
not as just a momentary event but as an enduring presence. For
reasons unfathomable, we stumble into the land of "trouble."
Suddenly, there we are in a world where "things are not as we
had hoped they would be." When trouble takes the form of
violating assault, it knocks everything off kilter, making the
future a problem because the present is a problem. Painfully,
this trouble is not something from which we ever fully recover.
The damage it causes is real and often permanent—even if, in
the short term, we find ways to manage the fallout. This fall is
not just social or collective; it also structures the deep logic of
our interior worlds, its rupturing force reaching into our core.

In this way, we are set up to relentlessly mourn the loss of our own innocence, whether at our own hands or another's; it is gone and it will not return. We constantly grieve the loss of ourselves while discovering our innocence. What fortitude of spirit this demands from us.

❧❧❧❧❧

Sin-grace as gestures of imagination? At the edge of every thought, there resides the promise of both ever-deepening loss and insistently imposed newness. Mourning and wonder. There, at the edge of every eyeblink, every muscle bend, and every lip-formed moment of speech—there is a space that both carries traumatic loss and yet remains open and new. Poised here, we always wait to be dragged from despair into light. The cross trains us in these dispositions of body and imagination. It narrates for us, again and again, two paradoxical stories about who we are: God's inevitably broken children, and God's constantly renewed beloved; these two stories run down parallel tracks of flesh and soul. They are not, however, driven toward evolving resolution. We are not becoming better or worse: we just are these two things, in the juxtaposed tension of our everyday life.

This is a profoundly presentist vision of life, landing us hard in the here and now: to be saved is not to be taken elsewhere. It is to be awakened—to mourn and to wonder. And to stand courageously on the promise that grace is sturdy enough to hold it all—you, and me, and every broken, trauma-ridden soul that wanders through our history. To us all, love comes.

Notes

Chapter 1: Trauma and Grace—Beginnings

1. See Cathy Caruth, *Unclaimed Experience: Trauma, Narrative, and History* (Baltimore: Johns Hopkins University Press), 1996.

2. The image also makes it clear that trauma does not just refer to the moment in which an injury first happens. As in the case of a cut or a bruise, the damaged tissue of a wound can stay with you long after the initial event passes and may actually even grow worse with time if it is not attended to properly. In the same way, traumas are not just momentary events: the lifespan of most wounds extends over time and wounds require care if their effects are to pass.

3. For the purpose of this book, I have chosen to focus on events and situations about which there is little debate as to their "violent" character. I realize that by using these examples, I am sidestepping legitimate questions about what makes an event "violent" and whether or not a universal definition can be generated.

4. Donald Kalsched, *The Inner World of Trauma: Archetypal Defenses of the Personal Spirit* (New York: Routledge, 1966), 2, developed notion of the unbearable.

5. This quote from Hofer was cited in G. Rosen, "Nostalgia: A Forgotten Psychological Disorder," *Psychological Medicine* 5 (1975): 342–47, http://www.psychosomaticmedicine.org/cgi/reprint/55/5/413.pdf. In his dissertation, Hofer famously coined the term "nostalgia" to translate *Heimweh* into a medical condition of homesick soldiers. Also see related works such as Bessel A. van der Kolk, Alexander C. McFarlane, and Lars Weisaeth, eds., *Traumatic Stress: The Effects of Overwhelming Experience on Mind, Body, and Society* (New York: Guilford Press, 2007).

Chapter 2: 9/11's Emmaus

1. Bessel A. van der Kolk expertly recounts a hundred years of evolving concepts in his article "Posttraumatic Stress Disorder and the Nature

of Trauma," *Dialogues in Clinical Neuroscience: Posttraumatic Stress Disorder* 2, no. 1 (2000): 7–22.

2. Ibid.

3. Kali Tal, "There Was No Plot and I Discovered It by Mistake: Trauma, Community and the Revisionary Process," in *Worlds of Hurt: Reading the Literatures of Trauma* (New York: Cambridge University Press, 1996), chap. 6.

4. Maya Angelou, *On the Pulse of the Morning* (New York: Random House, 1993), stanza 7.

5. See the quotation from Hofer on p. 20.

6. Lawrence Langer, *Versions of Survival: The Holocaust and the Human Spirit* (Albany: State University of New York Press, 1982), 88.

Chapter 3: Soul Anatomy

1. I want to thank Susan Pfeil, whose course work on Calvin, the Psalms, and trauma theory played a crucial role in helping me conceptualize the central argument of this essay.

2. John Calvin, *The Institutes of the Christian Religion*, ed. John T. McNeill, trans. Ford Lewis Battles, 2 vols., Library of Christian Classics 20–21 (Philadelphia: Westminster Press, 1960).

3. John Calvin, *Commentary on the Book of Psalms*, trans. James Anderson, 5 vols. (Edinburgh: Calvin Translation Society, 1845). The commentary is a work of mammoth proportions, comprising five volumes. Calvin originally wrote it in Latin and published it, near the end of his life, in Geneva, in 1557. The text was translated into French and published in 1563; as early as 1571 we find it translated into English and being distributed widely. Much of the commentary originated as lectures he delivered in Geneva between 1553 and 1557. See James A. De Jong, "'An Anatomy of All Parts of the Soul': Insights into Calvin's Spirituality from His Psalms Commentary," in *Calvinus Sacrae Scripturae Professor: Calvin as Confessor of Holy Scripture; Die Referate des Congrès International des Recherches Calviniennes, International Congress on Calvin Research, Internationalen Kongresses für Calvinforschung, vom 20. bis 23. August 1990 in Grand Rapids*, ed. Wilhelm H. Neuser (Grand Rapids: Wm. B. Eerdmans Publishing Co., 1994), 1–14. For additional discussions, see James Luther Mays, "Calvin's Commentary on the Psalms: The Preface as Introduction," in *John Calvin and the Church: A Prism of Reform*, ed. Timothy George (Louisville, KY: Westminster/

John Knox Press, 1990), 195–204; T. H. L. Parker, *Calvin's Old Testament Commentaries* (Philadelphia: Westminster Press, 1986).

4. For a fuller discussion of Calvin's rhetorical training and its influence on his understanding of theology, see Serene Jones, "Calvin and the Rhetorical Tradition," in *Calvin and the Rhetoric of Piety* (Louisville, KY: Westminster John Knox Press, 1995), 11–45.

5. Francis Higman, "Calvin the Writer," manuscript, Yale University, New Haven, CT, 1989.

6. Calvin, "The Author's Preface," in *Commentary on Psalms*, 1:xliv. For a broader discussion of the role of David in early modern literature, see Stephen Greenblatt, *Renaissance Self-Fashioning: From More to Shakespeare* (Chicago: University of Chicago Press, 1980), 118.

7. Calvin also identifies with the specific leadership challenges faced by David. As Calvin describes it, they both were caught in the midst of an ongoing social crisis in which they had to make life-and-death decisions without having the time they needed to reflect upon them. They both had to decide to take lives—to inflict violence on others—and did so "faithfully," even though they found it painful. They both faced constant betrayal by their closest friends and saw themselves as not just socially but also personally living in a state of constant siege and personal isolation. As they grappled with this, they both understood faith in God to be "not just a matter of cold reason" but, more important, a matter of a "warm heart." In this regard, Calvin celebrates the fact that David was emotional and not distant from the suffering around him, but immersed himself in it, and spoke to and about God out of it. See Calvin, "The Author's Preface," in *Commentary on Psalms*, 1:xxxix–xl, xliv–xlviii.

8. Barbara Diefendorf, *Beneath the Cross: Catholics and Huguenots in Sixteenth-Century Paris* (Oxford: Oxford University Press, 1991).

9. Calvin, *Commentary on the Psalms*, 1:72–73.

10. Calvin refers to his own refugee experience in his *Commentary on the Psalms*, preface and introduction.

11. In this regard, it is a text that had the capacity to speak not only to the profound spiritual challenges that violence raised for Calvin's community; it also addresses, in real and substantive ways, faith questions raised in a place like New Haven, Connecticut—as well as many other communities around the world—where the ongoing effects of debilitating violence are evident daily. In doing so, the text speaks across the centuries by bearing witness to the many ways in which harm done to persons affects how they view the world around them and their

understanding of God; even more important, the *Commentary on the Psalms* continues to speak to us by testifying to the ever-gracious and healing presence of God in the midst of such suffering.

12. Judith Herman, *Trauma and Recovery: The Aftermath of Violence—from Domestic Abuse to Political Terror* (New York: Basic Books, 1977), 52.

13. Calvin, *Commentary on the Psalms*, 3:409–10. Here Calvin uses *vulneratis* (wounded) for "trauma."

14. Ibid., 1:xxxvi–xxxvii.

15. Ibid., 3:416; cf. Rom. 8:22–23, 26–27.

16. Ibid., 1:xxxvii.

17. Herman, *Trauma and Recovery*, 155.

18. Shoshana Felman and Dori Laub, *Testimony: Crises of Witnessing in Literature, Psychoanalysis, and History* (New York: Routledge, 1992).

19. Calvin, *Commentary on the Psalms*, 1:xxxvii.

20. The three psalms I quote in the following three sections are psalms that were important to my church women's group, psalms we spent time interpreting. If I had chosen psalms solely based on Calvin's own selection method, the list would have been slightly different.

21. Calvin, *Commentary on the Psalms*, 1:xxxvii.

22. See, e.g., ibid., 1:xlii.

23. John Calvin, "Articles Concerning the Organization of the Church and of Worship at Geneva Proposed by the Ministers at the Council, January 16, 1537," in *Calvin: Theological Treatises*, trans. J. K. S. Reid (Philadelphia: Westminster Press, 1954), 48.

Chapter 5: The Mirrored Cross

1. In both tales, there is also an ongoing debate about whether the theory of language one generates from the founding event can be applied usefully to all experiences or just to those that obviously share in the form of that originating moment. In trauma theory, this is the debate over whether every time language is used, traumatic absence is invoked. In theology, this debate revolves around the status of natural theology in relation to the unknowability of God.

Chapter 6: The Unending Cross

1. "Performance criticism" is a term that David Rhoads, of the Lutheran School of Theology at Chicago, has coined to describe an emer-

gent approach in biblical studies. We draw here upon his paper "Performance Criticism: A New Methodology in Biblical Studies?" unpublished manuscript, 2004, 4; cf. "Performance Criticism: An Emerging Methodology in Biblical Studies," paper presented at the annual meeting of the Society of Biblical Literature, Philadelphia, November 21, 2005, http://www.sbl-site.org/assets/pdfs/Rhoads_Performance.pdf, 26.

2. By "performer" I mean one who recites from memory, improvising on a story line, or reading aloud from a manuscript. All are conventions appropriate to the cultural expectations of the time for the performance of literature.

3. Alan L. Boegehold, *When a Gesture Was Expected: A Selection of Examples from Archaic and Classical Greek Literature* (Princeton, NJ: Princeton University Press, 1999), 5.

4. This story was recited by Richard Ward in the original lecture that this section is based upon. His well-honed storytelling skills have never ceased to amaze as much by way of what they physically perform as by way of what they say. Hence, Ward's insight into gesture, the spine of this section, emerged from an embodied practice more than from studies of systematic theology.

5. Thomas H. Troeger, "Solid Meanings Unfold: The Terror of Resurrection," *Lexington Theological Quarterly* 36, no. 2 (Summer 2001): 69.

6. John Dominic Crossan, *The Historical Jesus: The Life of a Mediterranean Jewish Peasant* (San Francisco: HarperSanFrancisco, 1991), xi.

Chapter 7: Sin, Creativity, and the Christian Life

1. This chapter was originally cowritten with Cynthia Rigby. I am deeply indebted to her for the collaboration that generated the ideas in this essay and for her work in formulating and writing them with me. Her words, her thoughts, her arguments, and her spirit thoroughly saturate these pages.

2. As cited by William A. Dyrness, *Visual Faith* (Grand Rapids: Baker Academic, 2001), 90.

3. Ibid.

4. Belden Lane, "Fantasy and the Geography of Faith," *Theology Today* 50, no. 3 (1993): 400, http://theologytoday.ptsem.edu/oct1993/v50-3-article5.htm. We are indebted to Reno Lauro for directing our attention to von Balthasar and Lane.

5. See Valerie Saiving, "The Human Situation: A Feminine View" (*Journal of Religion*, April 1960), in *Womanspirit Rising: A Feminist Reader in*

10. For example, numerous twentieth-century theologians (Rahner, Tillich, Reinhold Niebuhr) have assumed that the quality of "self-making" is an essential feature of personhood before God. Recent work in the area of theology and disabilities has provided a much-needed assessment of the limits of such language and its roots in a discourse of "efficient production."

11. See Dorothy E. Roberts, *Killing the Black Body: Race, Reproduction, and the Meaning of Liberty* (New York: Pantheon Books, 1997); Patricia Hill Collins, "A Comparison of Two Works on Black Family Life," *Signs* 14, no. 4 (Summer 1989): 875–84.

12. On reproductive loss and technology, see Lisa Cartwright, *Screening the Body: Tracing Medicine's Visual Culture* (Minneapolis: University of Minnesota Press, 1985).

13. See Lynn M. Morgan and Meredith W. Michaels, eds., *Fetal Subjects, Feminist Positions* (Philadelphia: University of Pennsylvania Press, 1999).

14. Although I include infertility in my discussion of reproductive loss, the "thick description" I offer here addresses more directly experiences of miscarriage and stillbirth.

15. A compelling account of the interplay between powerlessness and guilt is given in Beth Powning's *Shadow Child: An Apprenticeship in Love and Loss* (New York: Carroll & Graf Publishers, 1999).

16. For an excellent discussion of the relation between hope and conceptions of selfhood, see William F. Lynch, *Images of Hope: Imagination as Healer of the Hopeless* (Baltimore: Helicon Press, 1965).

17. See the next note.

18. See Linda L. Layne, "Breaking the Silence: An Agenda for a Feminist Discourse of Pregnancy Loss," in *Feminist Studies* 23, no. 2 (Summer 1997): 289–315.

19. Here I refer to feminist theorists such as Susan Moller Okin, *Justice, Gender, and the Family* (New York: Basic Books, 1989); Alison Jaggar, *Feminist Politics and Human Nature* (Totowa, NJ: Rowman & Allanheld, 1983); and Carol Gould, *Rethinking Democracy: Freedom and Social Cooperation in Politics, Economy, and Society* (Cambridge: Cambridge University Press, 1988). Also see Rosalind Pollack Petchesky, *Abortion and Women's Choice: The State, Sexuality, and Reproduction*, rev. ed. (Boston: Northeastern University Press, 1990).

20. Here I include theorists such as Carol Gilligan, *In a Different Voice: A Psychological Theory of Women's Development* (Cambridge, MA: Harvard University Press, 1982); Carol Gilligan, ed., *Mapping the Moral*

Domain: A Contribution of Women's Thinking to Psychological Theory and Education (Cambridge, MA: Harvard University Press, 1988). See also Mary Jeanne Larrabee, ed., *An Ethic of Care: Feminist and Interdisciplinary Perspectives* (New York: Routledge, 1993); Nel Noddings, *Caring: A Feminine Approach to Ethic and Moral Education* (Berkeley: University of California Press, 1984); Martha Alberton Fineman, *The Neutered Mother* (New York: Routledge, 1995).

21. For a fuller discussion of this assessment of the material origins in feminist theory, see Lynne Huffer, *Maternal Pasts, Feminist Futures: Nostalgia, Ethics, and the Question of Difference* (Stanford, CA: Stanford University Press, 1998).

22. The best-known representative of this perspective in feminist theory is Julia Kristeva. See her "Revolution in Poetic Language" and "Stabat Mater," in *The Kristeva Reader*, ed. Toril Moi (New York: Columbia University Press, 1986), 90–136, 160–86.

23. For general feminist discussions of the place of tragedy in feminist theory and theology, see Kathleen Sands, *Escape from Paradise: Evil and Tragedy in Feminist Theology* (Minneapolis: Fortress Press, 1994).

24. For an account of Mary that briefly covers each of these perspectives on her, see Mary Aquin O'Neill, "The Mystery of Being Human Together," in *Freeing Theology: The Essentials of Theology in Feminist Perspective*, ed. Catherine Mowry LaCugna (San Francisco: Harper, 1993), 139–60. Also see Marina Warner, *Alone of All Her Sex: The Myth and the Cult of the Virgin Mary* (London: Weidenfeld & Nicolson, 1976).

25. Serene Jones, *Calvin and the Rhetoric of Piety*, Columbia Series in Reformed Theology (Louisville, KY: Westminster John Knox Press, 1995).

26. See Luce Irigaray, "La Mysterique," *Speculum of the Other Woman*, trans. Gillian C. Gill (Ithaca, NY: Cornell University Press, 1985), 191–202.

27. This particular issue (and its thematic implications) runs through Jürgen Moltmann's *The Crucified God: The Cross of Christ as the Foundation and the Criticism of Christian Theology* (San Francisco: Harper & Row, 1973).

Chapter 9: Mourning and Wonder

1. See Lawrence Langer, *Versions of Survival: The Holocaust and the Human Spirit* (Albany: State University of New York Press, 1982), 88.

CPSIA information can be obtained
at www.ICGtesting.com
Printed in the USA
LVHW01s2333080518
576541LV00001B/9/P

9 780664 234102